EATING DISORDERS

How to Recover Effectively from Anorexia, Bulimia, and Binge Eating

COMPREHENSIVE HEALTHCARE RESEARCH

© Copyright 2021—All rights reserved.

It is not legal to reproduce, duplicate, or transmit any part of this document in either electronic means or in printed format. Recording of this publication is strictly prohibited and any storage of this document is not allowed unless with written permission from the publisher except for the use of brief quotations in a book review.

Contents

Introduction	v
1. WHAT IS AN EATING DISORDER?	1
Anorexia Nervosa	2
Bulimia Nervosa	10
Binge Eating Disorder	17
Disordered Eating	23
Eating Disorder Prognoses	24
Comorbid Disorders	27
2. LESSER-KNOWN EATING DISORDERS	37
OSFED	38
Orthorexia Nervosa	47
ARFID	51
Pica	56
Diabulimia	59
Rumination Disorder	63
3. EATING DISORDER CAUSES	73
Genetic Factors	74
Biological Factors	75
Psychological Factors	76
Sociocultural Factors	78
4. WHO GETS EATING DISORDERS?	87
Eating Disorders: Who Gets Them?	88
Eating Disorder Demographics	90
Pro-Ana and Pro-Mia Websites	95
Are Eating Disorders Preventable?	95
5. TREATMENT OPTIONS	103
Treatment Options: An Overview	104
Choosing Outpatient Treatment	106
Choosing Inpatient Treatment	111
A Day in the Life of Residential Treatment	117
Therapeutic Treatment Options	122

6. INTUITIVE EATING 133
   What Is Intuitive Eating? 134
   What Are the Principles of Intuitive Eating? 134

7. IS RECOVERY POSSIBLE? 143
   What Is the Difference Between *Recovery* and *Recovered*? 144

   Final Words 149
   References 151

Introduction

Eating disorders do not discriminate.

In 2020, it was estimated that 20 million women and half as many men in the United States alone either struggled or continued to struggle with an eating disorder.[1] Worldwide, the number is much larger, affecting at least 9 percent of the total population.[2] If these numbers seem surprising, you aren't be alone in feeling that way: eating disorders can be insidious, so much so, they can develop without us even realizing. They can also be enticing in a dark, alluring fashion that can be irresistible to the women, men, teens, and children who are predisposed to developing eating disorders.

Within the pages of this book, we will examine the ins and outs of eating disorders, from defining each of the major disorders and their symptoms to discussing whether or not recovery from such debilitating conditions is possible, as there is some debate about this among those with eating disorders. We will unravel the many mysteries behind eating disorders through qualitative and quantitative data and research, and do our utmost to leave you feeling as though you have a better grasp on the causes, symptoms, psychology, and treatment options available for those with eating disorders. If you or a loved one suspects they may have an eating disorder, you will find use in this book for you as well: we'll be exploring resources available to those suffering from eating disorders throughout each chapter.

Finally, we will meet seven young men and women who have survived their own eating disorders and provide a glimpse into the world of what it is truly like to live with a condition that eats one from the inside out. They will illustrate from a first-person perspective what it feels like to develop, fall into the grips of, and recover from an eating disorder. It is important to remember that no two stories are quite alike, and that many recovery stories are not quite linear. We will dive into the trajectory of recovery later on in the book, but for now, keep in mind that our testimonials are for educational purposes and should not be viewed as the end all be all of what an eating disorder looks like.

Eating disorders, if left unchecked, can be deadly. But this book serves as a reminder that, given the proper resources, information, and treatment, recovery is possible. It can be elusive and extremely difficult to achieve, sometimes taking years or even decades before one finds their way back to a path of balanced psychological health, but it is out there. Simply read on to discover how.

ONE

What Is an Eating Disorder?

WHEN DOES a diet stop being just a diet? Is there an invisible line in the sand that can be crossed, a point of no return, that can doom a person to having an eating disorder?

One of the many difficult features about eating disorders is that there is no simple answer to these questions. Even though eating disorders are known to be the deadliest of all mental illnesses, no one knows for certain what is the root cause of an eating disorder. A combination of genetic, biological, psychological, and sociocultural factors are theorized to be behind these deleterious conditions, though more research is needed to get to the bottom of what makes eating disorders take hold.

So, what is an eating disorder, and how would you know if you had one? According to the American Psychiatric Association, eating disorders are defined as acute and lasting disruptions in eating behaviors, which are accompanied with high levels of emotional and psychological distress.[1] To provide you with an example, being on a juice cleanse isn't easy, but someone with an eating disorder takes any diet to the extreme. When an individual has an eating disorder, they might start *off* on a juice cleanse, but the cleanse quickly becomes an obsession with weight loss, body image, and even a sense of worthiness as a human being. There is a misconception that having an eating disorder means that one solely has an interest in losing weight, but this is, by and large, a farce. The truth of the matter is that eating disorders are enormously complex, and have a multitude of facets that require much more research and funding than many in the eating disorder community believe they have been given thus far.

Now that you've been given something of an introduction to what an eating disorder is, it's time to delve into three of the most commonly known eating disorders: anorexia nervosa, bulimia nervosa, and binge eating disorder. We will discuss the signs, symptoms, and prognosis for each of these disorders. Let's begin with anorexia, which is perhaps the most well-known out of the three.

Anorexia Nervosa

Anorexia nervosa is what most people might picture when they imagine an eating disorder, though not everyone who has anorexia experiences it in the same way. Anorexia is distinguished by extreme weight loss that results in inappropriate weight for one's height, build, age, and—in many, but not all individuals—a distorted sense of body image known as *body dysmorphia*. Body dysmorphia can affect people who do not have eating disorders at all, but the experience is the same: it causes the afflicted person to have a warped, often negative, perception of their body that does not align with reality. For someone with anorexia nervosa and body dysmorphia, they will perceive themselves as having a much larger body shape than what they actually have. No matter how much weight they lose, they will see an overweight person in the mirror, which for many people with eating disorders is a nightmare. Although less common, there are instances when those with anorexia know exactly how frail they have become, but lack the physical and psychological capability to stop losing weight.

Anorexia nervosa is characterized by more than simply thinking one is fat and seeing a reflection that confirms as much. There are a number of behaviors that go into having anorexia, which are often heavily restrictive or ritualistic in nature. In order to be diagnosed with anorexia nervosa, one must meet the following criteria as described by the *Diagnostic and Statistical Manual of Mental Disorders*, the most updated version of which is known as the DSM-5. The DSM-5 states the following criteria for anorexia:

1. Restriction of energy intake relative to requirements leading to a significantly low body weight in the context of age, sex developmental trajectory, and physical health.
2. Intense fear of gaining weight or becoming fat, even though underweight.
3. Disturbance in the way in which one's body weight or shape is experienced, undue influence of body weight or shape on self-evaluation, or denial of the seriousness of the current low body weight.[2]

Notably, there are subtypes of anorexia nervosa that are worth mentioning here, not least of which is atypical anorexia. *Atypical anorexia* is defined as individuals who would otherwise meet the criteria for anorexia if it weren't for their current weight; they are not underweight, despite losing a significant amount of weight.[3] Atypical anorexia can be tricky to catch and even trickier to diagnose, especially due to the fact that it can appear in people who are at an appropriate weight for their height and stature. One of the things that makes it so sneaky is the pervasive diet culture that makes eating disorders so prevalent. When someone is overweight and mysteriously drops pounds off of their frame, friends, family, and coworkers praise them and demand to know their secret. Sometimes, the secret is a healthy, balanced diet and a new exercise regimen. Other times, that secret is atypical anorexia or another eating disorder.

There are two other subtypes of anorexia nervosa, which are generally more widely recognized than atypical anorexia: the restrictive subtype and the binge-eating/purging subtype. The *restrictive subtype* is perhaps more well-known than the binge-eating/purging subtype, as it is what many people may think of when they picture an individual who is suffering from anorexia. As the name suggests, they will greatly restrict their food intake —sometimes fluid intake as well—for the purpose of losing weight. Oftentimes, overexercise is also involved. Someone with the restrictive subtype of anorexia nervosa may fast for days at a time, or eat only small amounts to get by, or try many types of diets in an attempt to lose as much weight as possible.

An individual struggling with the *binge-eating/purging subtype* of anorexia will have a different experience. They will still be dangerously underweight, but will engage in behaviors such as binge eating (which we will explore later on), abusing laxatives as a means of losing weight, and using diuretics in an attempt to get rid of the water weight in their bodies so that they may, again, weigh as little as possible. It is also very common for those with anorexia nervosa—and eating disorders in general—to have an obsession with weighing themselves, sometimes several times a day to monitor any minute changes that take place. But what other behaviors and rituals are characteristic of anorexia, and how can you recognize if you or a loved one is at risk for developing the disorder? Besides seeing a distorted image of oneself in the mirror and repeated weighing, what does it look like when someone has anorexia?

Anorexia can vary greatly from person to person, but there is a wide range of signs and symptoms that you can look for when trying to determine if you or someone you know is suffering from the disorder. The following lists (courtesy of the National Eating Disorders Association website, if you would like more information) can help you to identify whether you or someone in your life might be on the verge or already in the grips of anorexia:

Physical Signs

- Dramatic weight change has occurred. As we addressed earlier in the case of atypical anorexia, this may not always look unhealthy, so be cognizant of other symptoms as well.
- Fainting (from lack of nutrition).
- Gastrointestinal distress.
- Dry skin and brittle nails (also from a lack of nutrition).
- In women, menstrual cycle irregularities or cessation may take place as the reproductive system begins to shut down and hormonal imbalances occur. We will discuss the physical costs of eating disorders later within this chapter.
- Impaired immune system.
- Lower overall body temperature, causing one to feel cold regardless of the weather.
- Fine hair covering the body, otherwise known as *lanugo*. Some scientists think it is a reaction to the colder temperature of the body, and is a vain attempt to warm up.
- Dental issues, such as cavities and tooth erosion.
- Calluses and cuts on the back of knuckles and fingers as a result of repeated vomiting. This is present only in the binge-eating/purging subtype of anorexia nervosa, and also appears in other eating disorders such as bulimia nervosa.[4]

This list is not complete, as each individual with an eating disorder is distinct from each other despite having these commonalities. These are simply examples of things that one might expect out of someone who is struggling with anorexia or any of its subtypes. Next, we will move onto emotional signs, which, though they will not *necessarily* be what kills someone with anorexia, can still be extremely painful and must be taken into consideration:

Emotional Signs:

- Developing a strong need for control, particularly over food, exercise, and anything that has to do with either. Control is often a major theme in people who suffer from eating disorders, which we will dive into later on in this chapter.
- Having an intense fear of gaining weight despite being underweight.
- Thinking becomes rigid. There is no room for gray area any longer, and everything is black and white. This is what is called a *cognitive distortion*.
- Feeling a great sense of unworthiness and general malaise.
- May have comorbid disorders, such as depression, anxiety, obsessive compulsive disorder, post-traumatic stress disorder, and addiction. All of these, in conjunction with an eating disorder, can come to completely rule one's life and make someone's existence feel unbearable.[5]

Again, this is not a complete list, as everyone is vastly different and will experience anorexia in their own way, especially when it comes to their emotional well-being. The above are common experiences that many people with anorexia share, though they are by no means meant to be an ingredients list. Finally, we have the behavioral symptoms of anorexia nervosa. There are quite a few, and, unsurprisingly, can be quite variable.

Behavioral Signs:

- Withdrawing from friends and family and spending more time alone.
- Developing peculiar food rituals around mealtimes, such as the way one consumes food (cutting food up into tiny pieces, for instance).
- Wearing baggy clothes. The reason why someone might do this is debatable. For some, it can be to cover up how thin their starvation is causing them to become. For others, it can be to hide their body shape out of shame.

- Dressing in layers to hide thinness and to compensate for feeling cold from anorexia.
- Preoccupation with food, and everything that goes with food: weight loss, dieting, exercise, and the like. Some people with anorexia—and other eating disorders as well—may take up cooking for others, particularly decadent foods, and then neglect to partake in eating the food themselves.
- Making more and more excuses to avoid mealtimes or eating in front of others.
- Becoming obsessed with burning off all calories consumed. Not everyone with anorexia nervosa develops an exercise addiction, but it is a common method of ridding oneself of any unwanted food they've consumed if other types of purging are considered undesirable. We will cover purging more in the bulimia nervosa section.
- Having body dysmorphia concerning body weight or shape, as discussed previously.
- Cutting out entire food groups is a major sign to look out for if it appears with any of the other symptoms from any of these lists. Those suffering from anorexia and other eating disorders come to fear food, to the point of certain foods—often those that are high in fat, calories, sodium, or other buzzword ingredients— being referred to as *fear foods*. If you or a loved one is developing fear foods, it can be a big indicator that something is wrong.[6]

These lists provide a more or less general overview of anorexia nervosa, and are not meant to be used to diagnose. If you are concerned about yourself or someone in your life, be sure to reach out for help immediately! Anorexia nervosa, if left untreated, can not only be miserable and debilitating, but fatal. It is estimated that somewhere between 5 and 20 percent of those who do not receive help for anorexia will not survive the disorder.[7] If that statistic is frightening, it should be. Anorexia is no joke and should be taken extremely seriously, even if you only suspect that you or someone you care about is beginning to slide down the slippery slope into anorexia's grip. We will provide plenty of resources and advice for how to go getting help later on in this book, so if you feel stuck or uncertain, don't worry: you are in safe hands.

We have defined anorexia nervosa, described its three subtypes, and covered some of the signs and symptoms that can be used to identify if you or someone you know is struggling with anorexia. Now, it is time to discuss the health consequences of having anorexia. Although such things can be scary to read about, they are important to go over because they highlight the true cost of developing an eating disorder. It is easy to see eating disorders as glamorous—especially anorexia, since it is particularly prevalent in the modeling industry and is therefore one that women (and increasingly men) are bombarded with in the media. However, the price of starvation, overexercise, and binge/purge cycles can be terrible. Without exaggeration, it is almost as though those with eating disorders give their lives to the disorder: they may be willing to lose everything in order to support their behaviors. If this sounds similar to a drug addiction, you are onto something, but we will come back to this in a bit. For now, let us focus on what happens to the human body when it is battered by an eating disorder like anorexia nervosa.

Health Consequences of Anorexia Nervosa:

- Osteoporosis/osteopenia, or thinning of the bones. This, like many consequences of anorexia, is a result of poor nutrition. Unfortunately, unlike some other health effects of anorexia, osteoporosis and osteopenia are irreversible. Having brittle bones can put one at a higher risk for certain cancers and fractures, even at a young age.
- Vitamin and mineral deficiencies.
- Liver problems as a result of rapid weight loss. Losing weight too quickly is detrimental to one's internal organs and can cause damage.
- Gallstones, which may need to be removed through surgical intervention if they cannot be passed.
- Lean muscle loss. This may not sound particularly life-threatening, and it isn't. However, it is still harmful to the body's general build and chemistry to lose muscle mass.

- Loss of elasticity in the skin due to the body shrinking more quickly than the skin can keep up. This problem is almost preposterous, but it can cause even poorer body image in eating disorder sufferers and increase the drive to lose even more weight to compensate.
- Dehydration. Sometimes, as previously mentioned, those with anorexia restrict fluids as well as caloric foods, which can lead to such severe dehydration that it can result in hospitalization. Dehydration can also happen as a result of purging.
- Deterioration of the internal organs, especially the heart and kidneys (and liver). The body begins to digest all nonessential tissues in an attempt to keep itself alive as starvation progresses, and then, once all nonessential tissues are gone, the essential ones start to go too.
- Loss of menstruation and lowered testosterone levels.
- Mental health and other psychological disturbances, including addiction. It is very common for those struggling with anorexia nervosa and other eating disorders to develop comorbid disorders such as depression, anxiety, OCD, alcoholism, drug addiction, or a mixture of the above. We will cover why this is the case later on in the chapter after we finish discussing the details of bulimia nervosa and binge eating disorder.[8]

Clearly, anorexia is not only a vicious disease of the mind, but it wreaks havoc on the body. It does more than simply cause someone to lose weight: it can permanently damage their bones and internal organs, not to mention their mind. While recovery is possible for those who receive treatment for anorexia, it is an arduous process that requires commitment and often a whole team in the form of friends, family, and medical professionals who are willing to provide love and support to help see the anorexic individual through.

We have shed some light on the dark world of anorexia nervosa, so now it is time to turn the spotlight over to the next eating disorder on our list: bulimia nervosa. Bulimia does not often receive as much attention as anorexia does, at least not in popular media, so we will do our due diligence to provide as much information as possible about it here, to be sure that you come away feeling educated on the subject.

Bulimia Nervosa

Bulimia nervosa is the second most well-known eating disorder to the general public. It is not typically as romanticized as anorexia nervosa, but it does maintain a popularity in certain online social circles (more on these particular circles will be covered in Chapter Three). Bulimia is characterized by a painful cycle of binging and purging behaviors. What are binging and purging?

When someone *binges*, they indulge in something to excess. This "something" does not necessarily have to be food, but someone with bulimia nervosa will consume vast quantities of food in one sitting, more than is appropriate for a single—or sometimes several—meals. They will then proceed to purge the food they have consumed, typically as quickly as possible so that they might rid themselves of the calories they have eaten. Binging is a compulsion and not a choice. We will talk more about what a binge feels like when we address binge eating disorder, but it is important to remember that when one has a binge, it is not due to a lack of willpower or a *desire* to eat as much food as one's body can hold; it's a powerful urge that demands to be sated, and it often will not go away until the bulimic gives in and binges. It isn't their fault, but it causes a great deal of shame, as well as a need to purge that is just as strong as the hunger to binge was.

Purging can take several different forms, some of which were mentioned when we discussed the binge-eating/purging subtype of anorexia nervosa. However, the primary and perhaps most popular form of purging (and arguably the most dangerous) is vomiting one's food. People who purge this way can become very adept at hiding what they are doing, developing special techniques to mask the sound and smell of their behaviors, such as throwing up in the shower or vomiting in plastic bags and storing them in odd places around the house for later disposal. This form of purging can, if left unchecked, be exceedingly harmful to the internal organs, particularly the esophagus and heart. Repeated vomiting will also lead to dental issues, often causing teeth to rot due to the constant introduction of stomach acid where it doesn't belong. This type of purging is particularly hazardous, as it can cause tears to form in the esophagus or even cause the esophagus to rupture while vomiting. It can even lead to cardiac arrest.

Other ways of purging include overexercise, which can also be quite dangerous; depending on the shape one's body is in, it can lead to the deterioration of muscles, loss of essential nutrients in the blood, electrolyte imbalances, and even sudden death, in severe cases. As we've already mentioned, someone hoping to purge might also abuse diuretics and laxatives, which they might use in addition to or instead of vomiting and overexercise. In truth, using diuretics and laxatives to lose weight is not effective to lose actual fat, and instead only serves to dehydrate the individual abusing them. This can cause gastrointestinal issues, as well as electrolyte imbalances that can potentially be deadly if left untreated. If you or someone you know is taking diuretics and laxatives with the intent to lose weight, you are reading the right book: you will find guidance here for how to effectively recover from your hardship, whether it is disordered eating or a full-blown eating disorder (there is a difference, as we will address later in this chapter).

Here is the DSM-5's criteria to classify bulimia nervosa:

1. Recurrent episodes of binge eating. An episode of binge eating is characterized by both of the following:

> Eating, in a discrete period of time (e.g. within any two-hour period), an amount of food that is definitely larger than most people would eat during a similar period of time and under similar circumstances.

> A sense of lack of control over eating during the episode (e.g. a feeling that one cannot stop eating or control what or how much one is eating).

2. Recurrent inappropriate compensatory behavior in order to prevent weight gain, such as self-induced vomiting, misuse of laxatives diuretics, or other medications, fasting, or excessive exercise.

3. The binge eating and inappropriate compensatory behaviors both occur, on average, at least once a week for three months.

4. Self-evaluation is unduly influenced by body shape and weight.

5. The disturbance does not occur exclusively during episodes of anorexia nervosa.[9]

Now is an important time to note that the "compensatory behaviors" that the DSM-5 outlines can be anything from the things we have covered (vomiting, overexercising, diuretics, laxatives) to embarking on crash diets and fasting. There are certain behaviors that are more closely associated with bulimia than others, which is why we have gone over them in detail, but it is crucial to keep in mind that purging—which is what is meant by a compensatory behavior—can come in many different forms. Bulimia nervosa can be more than the customary throwing up after meals, and it is pivotal to remember that it can, like anorexia nervosa, take many forms. The following are some of the signs and symptoms to look out for if you are worried that you or someone you know could be suffering from bulimia:

Physical Signs:

- Fluctuating weight. Many people with bulimia nervosa are not underweight, and may even be slightly overweight due to their binging behaviors. This does not, however, mean that they are any less at risk for any of the health consequences that tend to result from eating disorders, especially if the afflicted individual has been struggling for a long time.
- Gastrointestinal distress and stomach cramps.
- Fainting spells and dizziness.
- Cuts and calluses on the fingers and knuckles as a result of scraping the fingers against the teeth while vomiting.
- Swelling around the salivary glands or chubby "chipmunk" cheeks.
- Dental issues due to vomiting, including cavities and discoloration of the teeth.
- Sleep problems.
- Thinning of hair on head while growing lanugo elsewhere.
- Cold hands and swollen feet.
- Menstrual cycle irregularities in those who menstruate.[10]

As you can see, there are many similarities between anorexia and bulimia when it comes to the physical symptoms that one can experience. But what about the emotional impact of the illness? Unsurprisingly, there is quite a bit of overlap here, too.

Emotional Signs:

- Developing an intense need for control around food, weight loss, and body shape, just as is the case for anorexia nervosa.
- Feeling fearful of eating in public or around other people.
- Becoming overly concerned about appearance, perhaps making frequent comments about how one looks in comparison to others or remarking on imagined flaws.
- Experiencing extreme mood swings. Starvation and binge/purge behaviors can cause blood sugar and hormone levels to fluctuate, which makes it difficult to regulate mood and emotions.

- May have some or all of the comorbid disorders that were listed under anorexia: anxiety, depression, OCD, PTSD, and addiction.[11]

Eating disorders, while their presentations can be very different in terms of behavior, can clearly be nearly identical in terms of their emotional costs. This just goes to show that even though bulimia nervosa and anorexia nervosa are quite separate illnesses, eating disorders are all related through the ways they affect those who struggle with them. Of course, that isn't to say that someone wrestling with anorexia could necessarily be easily mistaken for someone who has bulimia. So how do you tell the two apart? The following are examples of some of the behaviors that an individual with bulimia might display:

Behavioral Signs:

- Disappearing to the bathroom soon after every meal. While this is not an indicator of bulimia all on its own, if you notice it combined with the other items on these lists, it could be a major red flag; the person in question may be purging their food.
- Creating an entire lifestyle around the binge and purge cycles that bulimia nervosa demands. This could mean making multiple trips to several different stores to discreetly stock up on food for a binge, or keeping a rigid exercise regimen for the purpose of burning off excess calories after eating.
- Frequently trying new diets in an attempt to lose the weight they fear may have been gained as a result of eating or binging. Dieting, while not generally the healthiest way to lose weight, is not a sign of an eating disorder or bulimia on its own, either, but holds plenty of potential to turn into a full-blown eating disorder in those who are predisposed to developing one.
- Withdrawing from friends and family.
- Becoming more militant with an exercise routine or starting one where there wasn't one previously.
- Developing purging behaviors, including any or all that we have covered above: vomiting, abusing laxatives and diuretics, overexercising, fasting, and so on.

- Engaging in binging behaviors, in which one might eat vast quantities of food at a time in a compulsive manner.
- Compensating for binges by skipping meals or taking smaller helpings than usual at mealtimes. The bulimic individual may also cut out snacking or desserts in a further attempt to lose weight, which may ultimately backfire in stronger urges to binge later on, furthering the cycle of the eating disorder.
- Beginning to steal or hide away food in places where it doesn't belong.
- Drinking water to excess, or other beverages that don't have calories. Sometimes this is done to make purging through vomiting smoother. Other times, it is done as a version of a meal replacement, especially if the drink is carbonated and can fill up the stomach. No matter what, it can be dangerous, as drinking too many fluids can cause imbalances in electrolytes, which can be extremely harmful and even fatal.[12]

While there is some overlap behaviorally between anorexia and bulimia, the two disorders are distinct from one another, and easy enough to differentiate between once you know what to look out for. However, make no mistake: though anorexia nervosa may be considered the most immediately dangerous of the eating disorders due to its effects on the body and the likelihood of its sufferers to commit suicide, bulimia nervosa can cause serious health consequences.

Health Consequences of Bulimia Nervosa:

- Issues with the cardiovascular system, namely the heart, as a result of eating too few calories.
- Gastrointestinal distress from starvation and overuse of laxatives and diuretics, if those are being abused as a means of purging.
- Potential for ruptured esophagus due to repeated vomiting, which is life-threatening.
- Electrolyte imbalances.
- Potential for the stomach to rupture due to binge eating, which is also life-threatening.

- Malnutrition from too much purging and restriction can lead to issues with the pancreas (pancreatitis).
- A wide variety of intestinal issues resulting from laxative and diuretic abuses, binging, and starvation cycles.
- Reproductive issues and lowered testosterone.
- Dry skin and brittle hair and nails.
- Deterioration of the internal organs, including the kidneys, liver, heart, and brain. All of these organs rely on nutrition and calories to function properly, and without them, they simply begin to shut down.
- Mental health and other psychological disturbances, including addiction.[13]

Bulimia nervosa is often looked at as the lesser of two evils. Sometimes, to someone who is completely ignorant of what they are about to get themselves into, it may even look like a brilliant solution to their emotional problems ("If I just stick my finger down my throat, I can eat anything I want, and then I'll finally be skinny!"). But bulimia is not a game, and it is not the way to lose weight. When people initially fall into an eating disorder, they rarely see it for the monster that it is . . . but we will catch a glimpse into that world at the end of this chapter when we meet Heidi. First, it's time to launch into our next eating disorder on our list: binge eating disorder.

Binge Eating Disorder

When most people picture an individual who has an eating disorder, they imagine a skeletal caucasian teenage girl. This is not only a myopic view, but it completely excludes anyone who has an eating disorder who might not be dangerously underweight (or underweight at all). It's not necessarily the fault of the general public that the depiction of a person suffering from an eating disorder that they have in their their heads is typically an anorexic one: anorexia nervosa is perhaps the most well-known out of the eating disorders, or at least some of its behaviors are the easiest to identify for someone who isn't familiar with the many features of an eating disorder ("Don't people with eating disorders just not eat?"). However, the truth of the matter is that not only do people with eating disorders eat, but depending on their eating disorder, they may sometimes eat too much. If someone is battling with the compulsive binging behaviors associated with *binge eating disorder*, eating might just be the problem.

We talked about bingeing in our section about bulimia nervosa, but saved the portion about the true drive and feeling behind a binge for binge eating disorder. For some, the disorder can feel like a switch that turns on and off the strong desire to eat.[14] It is important to remember that binges can be highly subjective, and that a binge to one individual may not seem like a binge to another; someone may devour a tray of lasagne meant for eight people while another might sneak an entire box of cereal. It's tough to compare these very different foods, but the emotion behind the binge is more crucial than the food that was consumed during the binge. While the DSM-5 will define binges as consuming larger than average amounts of food in short periods of time, the eating disorder community tends to focus more on how it *feels* when one eats to determine whether or not one binged. If you calmly listened to your hunger cues and needed to eat a whole box of cereal, that's one thing. But if that insatiable, compulsive need to eat beyond the level of comfortable fullness kicked in and forced your hand, that's quite another.

Some describe having a binge as a frightening, out-of-control experience in which one has to eat everything in sight and won't feel satisfied until there isn't anything left. There is always a terrible feeling of regret, shame, and worthlessness after a binge, but unlike those with bulimia, people with binge eating disorder don't purge their food. Instead, they must fight a losing battle with a disorder in which they feel compelled to binge, experience enormous guilt, and ultimately binge again to ease the burden of the awful emotions (or traumas) they are wrestling with. In short, binge eating disorder is experiencing utter powerlessness over food. Let's take a look at how the DSM-5 defines the disorder:

1. Recurrent episodes of binge eating. An episode of binge eating is characterized by both of the following:

> Eating, in a discrete period of time (e.g., within any two-hour period), an amount of food that is definitely larger than what most people would eat in a similar period of time under similar circumstances.
>
> A sense of lack of control over eating during the episode (e.g., a feeling that one cannot stop eating or control what or how much one is eating).

2. The binge eating episodes are associated with three (or more) of the following:

> Eating much more rapidly than normal.
>
> Eating large amounts of food when not physically hungry.
>
> Eating alone because of feeling embarrassed by how much one is eating.

Feeling disgusted with oneself, depressed, or very guilty afterward.

3. Marked distress regarding binge eating is present.

4. The binge eating occurs, on average, at least once a week for three months.

5. The binge eating is not associated with the recurrent use of inappropriate compensatory behaviors (e.g., purging) as in bulimia nervosa or anorexia nervosa.[15]

Binge eating disorder is a bit of a standalone disorder when it comes to eating disorders. It involves neither starvation nor purging nor any other compensatory behaviors, but this doesn't mean that it is any less debilitating to those who suffer from it. Binge eating disorder is perhaps the most invisible of the "big three" eating disorders that we will be exploring within this chapter, in that sufferers may not even realize that there is any help available to someone with their particular struggles. As we said at the opening of this section, there is really only one particular eating disorder group that is represented in the media, and it's not those with binge eating disorder.

Because binge eating disorder can be harder to identify, here are some signs and symptoms for you to look for if you're worried that you or someone in your life could have the disorder. As in the previous sections, these lists are not meant to be diagnostic tools, and should only be used for educational purposes.

Physical Signs:

- Fluctuating weight.
- Developing gastrointestinal issues, such as acid reflux or stomach pain.
- Cropping up of health issues related to "yo-yo dieting" or obesity.
- Difficulty concentrating, a nonspecific complaint that ails many eating disorder sufferers.[16]

If this list seems surprisingly short to you, it probably should serve to drive home the point that binge eating disorder is simply not as easy to spot as other eating disorders might be. In some ways, this is a shame: the more visible an ailment, the more likely it is to be treated. The squeaky wheel gets the grease, as the saying goes. While those with binge eating disorder may not necessarily be doomed to wrestle in silence with their illnesses, it is certainly not as infamous a disorder as anorexia or bulimia, though it does share some emotional commonalities with the two.

Emotional Signs:

- Feelings of worthlessness or low self-esteem. These emotions can become a binge cycle; no one develops an eating disorder because they love themselves, and that can snowball into the first binge, which causes guilt, which causes a binge, and so on.
- Becoming fearful of eating in public or around other people.
- Beginning to feel the need to withdraw from friends, family, and social activities.
- Starting to feel overly concerned about physical appearance, such as worrying that oneself will be looked at as "fat" by others.
- As with anorexia and bulimia, may suffer from one or more comorbid disorders.[17]

Plainly, there is some overlap here with our first two disorders. This is not to say, however, that binge eating disorder is not unique and that sufferers of the illness do not struggle within their own rite. These struggles primarily show up in the various behaviors of the disorder, a few of which are generally exclusive to binge eating disorder and not seen as much in other eating disorders.

Behavioral Signs:

- Stealing or storing food in peculiar places, such as bags, bedrooms, and in furniture. This behavior takes place for the same reason that it does in bulimia nervosa: to prepare for the next binge and to hide the behavior from others.

- Creating food rituals, just as someone with anorexia or bulimia would do.
- Eating alone in order to hide the amount of food that one is consuming at a time.
- Developing abnormal eating behaviors in addition to binging, such as dieting or *grazing* throughout the day. Grazing refers to a behavior in which an individual eats constantly as the day wears on.[18]
- Feeling disgusted or guilty with oneself after overeating, or even spiraling into a depression.
- Showing unreasonable concern with one's weight, shape, size, or appearance.
- Seeming uncomfortable eating around other people.
- Binging in secret repeatedly. A single episode of overeating is not enough to qualify as binge eating disorder, so if you find yourself worrying about overindulging once or twice on Thanksgiving, you're likely in the clear.[19]

While binge eating disorder can resemble bulimia in some ways, it is important to remember that there are no purging behaviors listed above. From the outside looking in (and to the untrained eye, especially if you are a concerned loved one) it can be difficult to tell the two apart due to the fact that the binging behaviors take place in secret and are not a public affair. No one with binge eating disorder wants to announce to the world that they have the disorder, as there is a great deal of shame involved in the feelings around a binge. However, arguably as costly are the potential health consequences of this illness. Although there may not be as lengthy a list as that of anorexia nervosa, some of them can still be severe if left untreated.

Health Consequences of Binge Eating Disorder:

- High blood pressure.
- High cholesterol.
- Heart disease.
- Weight gain or even obesity from repeated binging behaviors.
- Type 2 diabetes mellitus.

- Gallbladder Disease.
- Arthritis.
- Sleep apnea.
- Infertility or reproductive issues.[20]

Although it is less likely to do so on its own, binge eating disorder can still kill. Obesity can be dangerous, though it is not necessarily the beast that society might have us believe that it is. The term "obesity epidemic" is one that many of us are quite familiar with, as it has been hammered into our heads from books, television shows, movies, magazines, and sometimes our own loved ones, but it does more harm than good to group an entire body type with a term associated with disease. It's true that in some cases, being overweight can lead to health issues; this is well-documented in the medical community, and is a known side effect of the obesity that can result from binge eating disorder. However, it is imperative to keep in mind that not every large body is an unhealthy body! This is something that is stressed a great deal in the eating disorder recovery community, but is not as widely known by the general public, and it needs to be. Body Mass Index, or BMI, is largely irrelevant in determining whether or not someone is truly healthy. It was invented by a mathematician, not a physician, and he was more interested in creating data than he was in providing a comprehensive way to determine health based on weight.[21] The amount of fat that is on someone's body is not always indicative of their health, and it is easy for Western societies to confuse thin and skinny with healthy, which is simply not always the case.

Whether someone is suffering from binge eating disorder or anorexia nervosa, the effects of the disorders are devastating on both the mind and body. The many symptoms of having an eating disorder can leave one feeling pulled apart at the seams and desperate for help . . . but what if you don't have enough of the symptoms to qualify as having an eating disorder? You may still be struggling with body image or a restrictive eating pattern, but perhaps you don't meet the criteria that the DSM-5 claims is necessary to have an eating disorder. If this sounds like you, there is a title for that, too: disordered eating.

Disordered Eating

Although disordered eating is not considered to be an eating disorder in and of itself, it is still an issue to be taken seriously, as it can develop into a full-blown eating disorder. *Disordered eating* is defined as a wide variety of irregular eating habits and behaviors that resemble those of an eating disorder, but do not necessarily warrant an official diagnosis.[22] Oftentimes, individuals with disordered eating symptoms will be diagnosed with OSFED (Other Specified Feeding or Eating Disorder), or EDNOS (Eating Disorder Not Otherwise Specified), which is what OSFED used to be known as. However, disordered eating and OSFED are not the same thing (we will discuss OSFED in detail in Chapter Two), even though they can present similarly and ought to be differentiated.

It may be helpful to think of disordered eating as a precursor to an eating disorder in the same way that schizophrenia has a prodromal stage. It can be very easy to slip into a full-blown eating disorder from starting first in disordered eating, which can appear in any number of ways. For one person, it may be developing a negative body image and taking it out on a brand-new crash diet. For another, it may be sneaking fervent third helpings of dinner to bring back to his bedroom and binge on in secret later in the evening. The difference is that, in most cases, these behaviors don't occur often enough or with enough severity for them to be considered a "true" eating disorder.

This is not to say, however, that if you or someone you know is developing disordered eating it shouldn't be monitored or, better yet, you shouldn't reach out for help *as soon as possible*. While disordered eating does not always turn into an eating disorder and can resolve on its own, it is more likely to become something more serious than it is to get better on its own. Strongly consider getting help immediately if you suspect that you may have disordered eating; there is no such thing as playing it too safe when it comes to establishing a support team. We will cover this in depth in Chapter Four.

Eating Disorder Prognoses

The prognoses for various eating disorders vary. After all, no two eating disorders are quite the same, just as no two people struggling with their eating disorders are the same, even if they have an identical diagnosis. Thus, there is some variance in the prognoses of the eating disorders we have covered so far, as each medical team behind an afflicted individual has to take into account their emotional, physical, and mental conditions, in addition to factoring in the prognosis of their general eating disorder diagnosis. There is a great deal of data that goes into determining the prognosis of an individual with an eating disorder, as there is not a singular cause that usually drives a person to develop one. We will dive more into the causes of eating disorders in Chapter Three, but with that in mind, what are the survival rates of the eating disorders that we have discussed so far within this chapter? And how do you know if you or someone you love is likely to recover? In this section, we will go over the overarching prognosis of anorexia nervosa, bulimia nervosa, and binge eating disorder.

Anorexia Nervosa Prognosis:

The prognosis of anorexia nervosa, unsurprisingly, differs depending on the individual and a range of factors. These include length of the time spent with anorexia, the severity of the illness, and the type of treatment received to combat the illness.[23] Unfortunately, anorexia has the potential to be lethal if left untreated, and it's extremely important to catch it in its early stages to avoid a long, painful recovery process. It is a sad truth that those struggling with anorexia nervosa are five times more likely to die prematurely and eighteen times more likely to die of suicide.[24] This statistic is not meant to frighten, but is meant to educate, and perhaps spur to action. If you or someone you know is suffering, do *not* wait: get help as soon as possible. You could save a life.

However, on the subject of saving a life, it is possible that the anorexic individual may not want help or will not even recognize that they have a problem. The nature of an eating disorder can be all-consuming and can even seem to change someone's personality, turning them into a different person. Someone with anorexia may not want to follow their treatment plan or start treatment in the first place. Not everyone with anorexia nervosa experiences their eating disorder in this way—some are more than willing to recover when the concept is introduced. Whatever the case, the chance of recovery is higher the sooner that the individual receives help.

Finally, the probability of relapse for anorexia nervosa is distressingly high. This is not necessarily unique to anorexia, and is more of an eating disorder phenomenon in general. As we will discuss in the section on comorbid disorders later, eating disorders can be very addictive. Even so, there is hope for those suffering from anorexia if proper intervention is given (see Chapter Five to learn more) and there is commitment for recovery from the anorexic individual.

Bulimia Nervosa Prognosis:

The prognosis for bulimia nervosa tends to be a little better than that of anorexia nervosa, or at least it can be, if the illness in the afflicted individual was not quite as severe. Many of those who struggle with bulimia, if they receive treatment and ongoing support, will recover from their eating disorder. However, statistics show that while even though half of people with bulimia nervosa will make full recoveries, around 30 percent will recover partially, and approximately 10–20 percent will have ongoing struggles for the remainder of their lifetime.[25]

Just as is the case with anorexia, some people with bulimia may not want to receive treatment, or may not realize that there is a problem with their behaviors. It may seem almost ridiculous to suppose that someone can be making themselves vomit after mealtimes and not realize that there is an issue with what they are doing, but eating disorders mask the truth of the actions that individuals are performing, even to themselves. One of the key things to realize about *all* eating disorders—not just bulimia nervosa—is that they are very, very sneaky, and that this applies not only to how the eating disorders force individuals to act, but to the way they think as well. Eating disorders warp thinking patterns and thoughts, which is why, in part, those with these conditions can begin to seem like different people than they did before they had the disorder. If someone's thoughts, emotions, and behaviors are being disrupted by a disease, it can certainly affect their personality.

Even with this massive mental hurdle to jump over, those with bulimia nervosa have a chance at recovery if they are given the appropriate treatment and taught the skills to cope with the underlying emotional issues that, more likely than not, caused the disorder. There is still a high rate of relapse, but there is hope for bulimic individuals if they are committed to recovering and sticking to their treatment plan. If you or someone in your life is wrestling with symptoms of bulimia, get help right away.

Binge Eating Disorder Prognosis:

Overall, the prognosis for binge eating disorder is somewhat similar to that of bulimia nervosa. In one study, after around six years and time in treatment, more than half of people with the disorder recovered, one third had moderate success recovering, 6 percent did much more poorly, and 1 percent ran the risk of dying.[26] Clearly, binge eating disorder is not nearly as deadly (in general) as an eating disorder like anorexia nervosa, but that doesn't mean that it doesn't have its complications or dangers. We covered some of the health consequences of having binge eating disorder earlier on, but it can't be stressed enough that even if those with the disorder recover, they may suffer from other comorbid disorders that must be monitored in recovery as well (more on these next). Additionally, someone with binge eating disorder—or any eating disorder—may go on to develop a different eating disorder once they have given up the behaviors they once relied so heavily on to self-regulate. It is important to be sure that you or your loved one is receiving the proper support when tackling binge eating disorder, or it can pop up in the form of other eating disorders or different harmful behaviors rather than recovery.

One of the troubling aspects of battling any eating disorder—especially an eating disorder like binge eating disorder or bulimia nervosa—is that one cannot simply give up food in order to recover. Eating in a balanced, intuitive way that is aligned with your hunger cues is pivotal to living a normal life after an eating disorder, and banishing food from your life won't get you there. While an alcoholic must abstain from alcohol, a binge eater still has to eat; they simply must learn how to make peace with themselves while doing it. This is much more easily said than done, and can take many months or even years of dedicated work to achieve. But if the binge eater puts their mind and heart into it, their future is, more likely than not, a bright one.

Now that we have toured the prognoses of anorexia nervosa, bulimia nervosa, and binge eating disorder, it's time to look at some of the comorbid disorders that go hand in hand with eating disorders. There are many, and not every person with an eating disorder will have all—or any—of the disorders we discuss. Regardless, it is relevant to know why people with eating disorders tend to have multiple conditions at once, and what these conditions are.

Comorbid Disorders

There are a variety of comorbid disorders that someone might have at the same time as an eating disorder. A *comorbid disorder* is a condition that occurs alongside another condition. We provided some examples of these conditions back when we described some of the emotional signs of eating disorders, but to recap, they include (but are not limited to): depression, anxiety, OCD, PTSD, and addiction. While not everyone with an eating disorder will have a comorbid disorder, it is so common that we will be dedicating an entire section to some of the conditions that haunt eating disorder sufferers most.

Depression:

Depression can be completely debilitating all on its own, but when it is combined with an eating disorder, it may turn one's life into a living nightmare. When someone is depressed, their mood dips to levels beyond the threshold of what someone might recognize as ordinary sadness. Sadness and depression are not the same thing, and should not be confused for one another. When someone is sad, they may feel lackluster and sloweddown, but are capable of seeing that someday things will get better. When someone is depressed, however, they can lose all sense of hope that anything can improve, and it can drive them to self-injurious behaviors or even suicidality. In some cases, they may have a difficult time eating, sleeping, and taking care of themselves, and intervention may be needed. If someone is struggling with depression this severe on top of an eating disorder, life can not only be tough, but it can grind to a screeching halt.

It is not unusual for someone struggling with an eating disorder to feel melancholy or to sink into a depression as their eating disorder progresses. People suffering from eating disorders are already at an increased risk for suicide, and adding depression on top of their eating disorder diagnosis only increases that risk. If you or someone you know is grappling with eating disorder symptoms on top of depression, don't wait—reach out for help as soon as you can. You could alter or even save a life by doing so.

Anxiety:

Anxiety disorders and eating disorders are like siblings in the mental illness world: they are often found together. While it's normal for some level of anxiety and stress to visit anyone from time to time, if it becomes increasingly pervasive and begins to interfere with daily functioning, you may have an anxiety disorder to contend with, in addition to your eating disorder.[27] Anxiety feels differently from typical everyday stress, in that it may drive an individual to engage in bad habits to mitigate the negative feelings, or get so overwhelming that it causes panic attacks. When someone has both anxiety and an eating disorder, their anxiety may show up in the form of food rules ("I will only eat before noon today"), overexercise, or even self-harming behaviors.

Approximately 48–51 percent of those suffering from anorexia nervosa, 54–81 percent of people wrestling with bulimia nervosa, and 55–65 percent of those struggling with binge eating disorder will be diagnosed with an anxiety disorder in their lifetime.[28] Fortunately, there are many treatment options available for anxiety (and eating disorders, which we will explore in Chapter Five), so if you are getting to a point where being silent is no longer an option, there are many avenues for you to choose from when it comes to deciding which is right for you or someone you love.

Obsessive Compulsive Disorder (OCD):

Obsessive compulsive disorder is well-documented as co-occurring with eating disorders. When someone has obsessive compulsive disorder, they have unwanted obsessions that drive them to do repeated, compulsive behaviors.[29] It's true that many people without OCD complain about having repetitive behaviors in a casual, blasé fashion ("I'm just so OCD about the way I keep my silverware!"), but the reality of having OCD is much more laborious and intense. When it is present in the form of an eating disorder, the obsession takes the form of food and body image. Someone might have the strong desire to weigh out every gram of food that they consume, or cut their food into tiny pieces, or weigh themselves after every meal. Some people with obsessive-compulsive behaviors know that what they are doing is irrational, while others lack the insight to see that their behaviors are unusual and are causing them undue stress or harm.

OCD is an awful condition all on its own, and when it is combined with an eating disorder, as it so often is, it can become unbearable. It's important to seek the proper combination of treatment options for both if a return to a rich, full life is to be achievable.

Post-traumatic Stress Disorder (PTSD):

Post-traumatic stress disorder is another comorbid disorder that is likely to occur alongside any of the eating disorders we have discussed so far, and plenty of the ones we haven't. It is not unusual for eating disorders to be spurred by some type of trauma, which we will talk about in more detail in Chapter Three. PTSD is a chronic condition, and if it is not properly treated, it is likely that the symptoms will remain in the traumatized individual's life for years to come. There are three types of trauma that are recognized by the medical community: acute trauma, chronic trauma, and complex trauma. While experiencing trauma will not necessarily cause someone to develop PTSD, all people with PTSD have experienced at least one type of trauma.

When PTSD is combined with an eating disorder, it can make the road to recovery intricate and difficult. As with any comorbid disorder, there is an additional mental illness to address, and that can mean more medications, different therapies, and alternative treatment options. It's important to get to the root of the issue with both trauma and the eating disorder when treating either condition, and the two may wind up having very similar origins. If you or someone you love is suffering from PTSD and eating disorder symptoms, there is hope for recovery from both if you reach out for help and receive the proper support.

Addiction:

Addiction can be a deadly mental illness for anyone, but when they occur in someone with an eating disorder, they can be particularly hazardous. Up to 50 percent of those struggling with eating disorders run the risk of abusing alcohol or drugs during the course of their disorder.[30] Perhaps just as alarmingly, "during the course of their disorder" includes after their disorder, too; it is not uncommon for someone who has freshly recovered from an eating disorder to unwittingly pick up a new addiction.

Using the word *addiction* to describe an eating disorder is not an accident. Many of the behaviors that someone uses to maintain their eating disorder are highly addictive and are not to be taken lightly. For instance, exercise is touted as a healthy alternative to other negative coping mechanisms, and while this is absolutely true, for someone with an eating disorder, it can spiral from a coping skill to a compulsion. This is particularly evident in people with anorexia nervosa, though exercise addiction—which is a monster all its own—is evident in other eating disorders as well. The bottom line is that even though eating disorder behaviors do not always involve abusing a substance, they can be just as addictive and damaging as a substance abuse disorder, and just as lethal.

Although it is not necessary for an individual to abuse a substance for them to suffer from an addiction, many people with eating disorders do. The most popular drugs among those with eating disorders and substance abuse issues are laxatives, diuretics, emetics, amphetamines, heroine, cocaine, and alcohol.[31] They may take these drugs both to numb any emotional pain or to try to lose more weight. No matter what the reason behind the consumption, it is essential to treat both conditions early on in order to ensure a successful recovery. A dual-diagnosis of an eating disorder and an addiction is a tall order, and it has to be tackled as soon as possible.

We have defined what an eating disorder is, provided a look at some of the most well-known eating disorders, and have hopefully provided some insight into the often lonely reality of having an eating disorder. Now, it's time to take a look at what it's like to have an eating disorder through a personal narrative. Meet Heidi, a real woman who volunteered to share her story with you. Keep in mind that Heidi does not represent each and every eating disorder sufferer, and that her story is unique to her. But if you find commonalities between her tale and your own or someone you know, perhaps it can serve to help you feel less alone.

Heidi's Story

Heidi's aversion to friendships began as a toddler, which opened up the perfect window for a much darker, more deceitful type of relationship to blossom as she grew up: that with anorexia nervosa. Going to Appletree Daycare Center everyday was a miserable experience for young Heidi, and she had an extremely difficult time parting with her parents when it was time to be dropped off. For many children with similar experiences, it gets easier over time, but for Heidi, it never did. She knows now that what she was going through was the start of what would become debilitating social anxiety around her peers, which would ultimately motivate her to develop her eating disorder.

As you might imagine, elementary school was a nightmare for an anxious child like Heidi. She recalls becoming increasingly uncomfortable as she drew nearer to school, fighting her nerves all day while barely saying a word to a single soul, and desperately waiting until she could get home so she could finally relax. She was picked on and generally friendless until she managed to get in with a group of girls who were supposed to be her friends, but, reflecting back, never treated her like much of a friend. In every activity she was the last one to be chosen; if there was a playdate, she was only asked to come over if there was no one else available; and at birthday parties, she was forgotten. This is all to say that the stage was set perfectly for a hole to be left in Heidi's heart and psyche for a "friend" of sorts to worm its way in to comfort her in the best way she knew how: exercise.

Heidi's mother is an athlete. She runs a gym and a pool, is a personal trainer and marathon swimmer, and she had Heidi join the swim team when she was in elementary school. Heidi hated the swim team, but she developed an interest in other forms of fitness after watching her mother model them for her. After quite a bit of begging and pleading, Heidi's mother finally caved and created a special workout regimen for Heidi to do at the gym that was designed not to harm her growing child's body. Heidi recalls feeling cooler than cool marching into the gym to work out and get stronger at that age, and that feeling lasted as she transitioned into middle school. She continued to work out and build up her body and confidence in the gym, but as soon as she went to school, that confidence would vanish, and it was as though it had never existed. As other girls' bodies began to change, Heidi stayed thin in accordance to her natural physique. The girls in Heidi's class commented on how slim she was, and it bothered her to the point of her deciding to intentionally gain weight.

After some time of these behaviors, high school came around, and Heidi's efforts to pile on the pounds finally began to work. She describes herself as having no particular talents or place in her friend group, no cliched role to fall into that could have helped her to feel more confident. So, instead, she sunk further into the "too cool for school" attitude that she had been nursing since middle school, and that was that. Her sophomore year, she transferred to a private school where everyone had to wear the same uniform, and this made body comparison extremely easy. Heidi was blown away by the bodies of some of the girls in her new school, convinced that they were perfect and that hers was anything but. She also became visited by bouts of depression for the first time, which she had to contend with on top of her existing anxiety and growing hatred for herself and her body. When her depressive spells left her, her goal was always to lose more weight and work out harder.

Heidi has always hated school and learning due to the social aspect, but when high school ended, she decided to go to college anyway because she felt like she was supposed to. Her anxiety ramped up and she immediately turned to her security blanket of exercising to cope. She went to the gym, swam, and ran. A new behavior was added to the mix now that she was no longer home, and that was a new level of social anxiety surrounding mealtimes. She became extremely nervous navigating the dining halls, as they were filled to the brim with strangers, and survived the first few days before classes started at her new school on yogurt and apples that she could buy and eat in her room. As one might expect, she lost some weight, and the compliments began rolling in when she returned home the first time and everyone saw her "new" body. This created a cycle for Heidi in which she became terrified about gaining weight every time she was about to come back home for fear that she might not receive that same amount of praise. If she didn't return home thinner than the last time, she felt like a failure. It's easy to see how a thought pattern like this could become dangerous, and for Heidi, it did.

This went on for two years, during which time Heidi continued to lose weight, overexercise, and have intense anxiety surrounding eating and any trip home. She did not do very well in school this way, and began to fail her classes, which further contributed to her self-image of being unintelligent and completely useless at anything that wasn't diet- or exercise-related. It was no way to live, and things only got worse when her boyfriend unexpectedly got her pregnant in her junior year. She decided not to keep it, and her family was loving and supportive of her decision, but she was pregnant for nearly three months before she was able to find a doctor who was willing to perform the abortion. During this period, she gave herself permission to eat according to her cravings, as it was all she could do to fight the terrible nausea she experienced. As a result, she gained weight, and when the abortion was completed, she began to feel enormous guilt and shame for letting herself slip out of her typical diet. Her drive to lose weight returned once again, and it was straight back to the gym even though she should have been letting her body heal from the procedure.

COVID-19 struck while Heidi was at home "recuperating," and it gave her access to the 20,000 square foot gym that belonged to her family, which was closed to everyone but them. Anorexia nervosa sunk its teeth into this golden opportunity and Heidi jumped at the chance to exercise. In her own words: "My brain was in panic mode to lose weight, I would think to myself, 'Heidi, you have nothing but time and unlimited access to a gym and pool all to yourself, if you can't lose this weight you're a fucking loser and can't do anything.'" She describes the period of quarantine as adding fuel to the fire of her already unrealistic and extreme exercising habits, and it just served to make them worse. However, despite her exercising, her eating during this period remained relatively normal. She restricted when she could, but because she was living at home with her family again, it made it difficult for her to eat any differently than she would have in the past. She comforted herself with the knowledge that once she went back to school, she would be able to starve herself once again on top of her workouts to get the results she desired.

As Heidi fell deeper into her disorder, her depression returned like never before. She knew that there was something terribly wrong with her, and she wanted it to go away, but she didn't know what to do to save herself. She found clarity each time she visited the ocean, though there was a day when all she could do was sit there and cry, lost in her misery. It was time to tell her boyfriend, who she was still loosely seeing, what she was doing to herself. So, she did . . . and the results were not what she had hoped. He broke up with her, telling her that she had an eating disorder. Reflecting upon their relationship, Heidi knows now that it is for the best that the two of them are no longer together, but at the time, it stung to be left behind when what she needed was support.

Fortunately, Heidi did have support—it just came in the form of her family. She stopped trying to hide what she was doing around the house, though she kept going for a while, too afraid of what would happen to her mental state if she were to stop. And then she visited her doctor, who was "not very impressed" with what her eating and exercise habits were doing to her heart, and that marked the beginning of the end. After her trip to see her physician, she was no longer allowed to set foot in the family gym, go swimming in the pool, hike in the mountains near her home, or any other form of exercise. It made her absolutely inconsolable. She had never felt so depressed in her entire life, and wanted to die. She didn't care how she escaped her depression—she just wanted it to end.

Instead, Heidi wound up in a residential treatment center surrounded by caring staff and, for the first time in her life, loving friends who taught her what it was like to have genuine friendships. She committed to recovering from her eating disorder, and in doing so, her life began to change for the better. She graduated from residential to partial hospitalization, but when her best friend in treatment left prematurely and the environment in treatment began to focus too much on gossip and cliques, she decided to keep her head down and graduate as soon as she could from an intensive outpatient program. Her goal was to finish out strong, though there were many times when she was simply waiting to go home. When she did finally finish her program with all the tools she needed to succeed, Heidi left treatment with a new sense of hope for her future.

Today, Heidi is doing quite well overall. She admits that she is approaching the first point in her recovery where she could relapse if she isn't careful, but she *is* being careful, and her gentle approach with herself is carrying her through each day and into tomorrow. She is attending college again with an intent to transfer to a different university soon, and just received a well-earned B on a test, which flies in the face of the "I'm dumb and can't succeed in school" self-image she had built up for herself back in middle and high school. All in all, Heidi's story ends happily. She knows that she has control over how she views her life and looks at her eating disorder as something that may creep back up, but if it does, she will tackle it as it comes. Anorexia no longer has her in handcuffs, and for that, she is grateful.

Heidi's story ends in recovery, and provides a beacon of hope for anorexia nervosa sufferers who feel as though they may be trapped within their disorders and there is no chance of recuperation. It is always important to commit stories like hers to memory when researching anorexia, because so often we hear about those struggling with the disease who never quite get better, or who even pass away as a result of falling into the depths of the illness, and not everyone does. There are stories like Heidi's, which can serve to inspire and remind us that recovery is possible from anorexia and comorbid disorders like depression and anxiety, even if they are severe. As long as the desire to recover is there, it is attainable. And that is something to be enormously grateful for, indeed—just like Heidi is.

We will cover treatment options as a whole in Chapter Five, but if you or someone you know is suffering from depression or anxiety like Heidi and may be too scared to reach out to someone familiar or pick up the phone to call a hotline, you may be more comfortable with simply texting. Crisis Text Line is a hotline designed for specifically these sorts of scenarios. All you need to do is text HOME to 741-741, and a trained volunteer crisis counselor will help you to calm down and ease you through your time of need. If you find yourself too shy to utilize other people in your life for comfort and aid, Crisis Text Line could be a good resource to take advantage of. Don't let yourself live in torment from your emotions and eating disorder. There is absolutely no shame in asking for help, so be sure to do so before it's too late.

TWO

Lesser-Known Eating Disorders

HAVE you ever been compelled to eat objects that weren't food? Does the purity of your food matter to you above all else? If so, you aren't alone. You may have one of the eating disorders that we will cover within this chapter.

We know all about the disastrous effects of anorexia nervosa, bulimia nervosa, and binge eating disorder. There are movies and documentaries about this trio, but you will have a much more difficult time finding media coverage about a disorder like pica or orthorexia nervosa (both of which were described above). There are a variety of eating disorders that fall between the cracks of what the public views as an eating disorder, with behaviors that might seem strange and even outlandish from the outside looking in, but it is important to be sensitive to all of these conditions. Eating disorders come in all shapes and sizes, and now that we've learned about some of the more commonly diagnosed eating disorders, it's time to launch into an explanation of the disorders with which you may not be as familiar.

The eating disorders that we will be discussing within this chapter include OSFED, orthorexia, avoidant restrictive food intake disorder (ARFID), pica, and rumination disorder. We will cover them one by one much in the same way we did in the previous chapter, concluding with a testimonial of a man, Forest, who has survived a handful of these eating disorders. Let's begin with *OSFED*, which we encountered briefly in Chapter One and learned stands for *Other Specified Feeding or Eating Disorder*.

OSFED

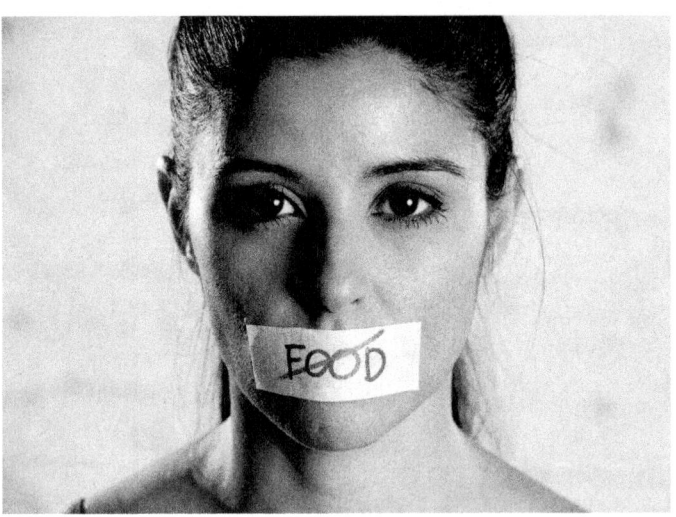

Apart from anorexia nervosa, some regard OSFED as the most dangerous of the eating disorders because it is the one that no one is likely to notice before it is too late to stop it from unfolding. OSFED, formerly known as *EDNOS*, or *Eating Disorder Not Otherwise Specified*, is sometimes regarded as the diagnosis that no one wants in the eating disorder community, as it is not seen by insurance companies as quite as severe a condition as some of the more widely known eating disorders. It is used as something of an umbrella diagnosis, as the symptoms are severe enough to be classified as an eating disorder, but don't fall under any other eating disorder category. Atypical anorexia is classified as OSFED, but that does not mean it is any less dangerous than anorexia nervosa. In fact, those with atypical anorexia have just as severe thoughts and behaviors as people with the DSM-5 diagnosable condition.[1]

There are several subtypes of OSFED, including—but not limited to— atypical anorexia (as we have mentioned), bulimia nervosa (of a low frequency and/or limited duration), binge eating disorder (of a low frequency and/or limited duration), purging disorder, and night eating syndrome. We will go over each of these in detail below, with the exception of atypical anorexia, which we covered in Chapter One. One important note to make before we begin is that we will not be covering the DSM-5 criteria for each subtype, though we will still describe each disorder and provide commentary:

Bulimia Nervosa (of a low frequency and/or limited duration) / Atypical Bulimia:

For this particular subtype of OSFED, all of the conditions of bulimia nervosa are met, but the binging and purging behaviors may be occurring with less frequency than with the DSM-5's criteria for bulimia, or the disorder has taken place over the course of less than three months (which, if you recall, it the minimum amount of time for a bulimia nervosa diagnosis). Someone with this form of bulimia will not binge and purge as often as someone with the full-blown disorder will, but this does not mean that they do not still have a serious eating disorder that is causing them significant mental and emotional distress.

Like atypical anorexia, atypical bulimia can fly under the radar and remain unseen by friends, family, and coworkers because the afflicted individual may not lose much weight even though they have developed an eating disorder and are struggling with seriously dangerous behaviors. Battling with negative body image and taking it out on oneself in the form of bingeing and purging is a path to certain disaster, and it can not only be difficult to spot, but it can ultimately turn into bulimia nervosa and the results can be lethal. If you or a loved one is beginning to show signs of atypical bulimia, there is never an inappropriate time to reach out for help. You could save someone from being claimed by bulimia nervosa further down the line.

Binge Eating Disorder (of a low frequency and/or limited duration) / Atypical Binge Eating Disorder:

Similar to atypical bulimia, this subtype of OSFED is characterized by behaviors—this time just binging—that either do not occur frequently enough or have not been happening for at least three months, as the DSM-5 stipulates. Atypical binge eating disorder is not to be confused with occasional overeating; it's important to remember the compulsive aspect to binge eating disorder that separates it from just an activity that someone might be able to turn on and off at will. Feeling a desire to have a second piece of birthday cake at your birthday party as a special treat probably isn't a sign of atypical binge eating disorder. If you feel driven to eat the entire cake in secret once all of the guests have gone home, this behavior could be indicative of an issue.

Even though the binging behaviors of atypical binge eating disorder do not occur with the same frequency as they do with the full version of binge eating disorder, they are still harmful to both the emotional and mental health of the individual carrying them out. An unfortunate side effect of binging can be weight gain, which can cause body image to plummet as the number on the scale climbs, and only worsen the cycle of binging. While binge eating disorder is not likely to kill on its own, it can be highly distressing to those suffering from it, and atypical binge eating disorder can present a gateway into this world of recurrent turmoil.

Purging Disorder:

Purging disorder may resemble bulimia nervosa or atypical bulimia to the untrained eye. However, even though someone with purging disorder may abuse laxatives, diuretics, exercise, vomit, or use other compensatory behaviors in order to control their weight or shape, they do not binge. As we covered in Chapter One when we discussed the health consequences of purging under the bulimia nervosa section, purging is extremely hazardous and can lead to a variety of issues in the body, including (but not limited to): electrolyte imbalances, esophageal ruptures, and even death. It can be tempting not to take purging disorder as seriously as anorexia, bulimia, or binge eating disorder because it may seem "incomplete" in terms of its symptoms, but it is still a grave eating disorder that needs recognition and care.

In cases of purging disorder, individuals are often not underweight and don't have enough symptoms of either anorexia or bulimia to be classified as having either one. In fact, the disorder is sometimes seen as a halfway point in between both.[2] Someone who spends a great deal of time purging might overuse gum or mints to cover up the smell of vomit, or, if they've been purging for quite a while, they may have developed Russell's Sign. *Russell's Sign* is the medical term used to describe cuts, calluses, and scars that can appear on one's fingers and knuckles from repeated forced vomiting using the hands. Individuals with purging disorder can also purge in other ways, such as using enemas inappropriately and too often. There are many methods that one might use to empty oneself of food, but each method is dangerous.

Although purging disorder is not widely known or recognized, those who have it know that it is very real. It is possible for sufferers of purging disorder to deteriorate into bulimia nervosa, which can be more severe and can have a worse prognosis than purging disorder does on its own. If you or someone you know is using compensatory behaviors to control your weight and shape, be sure to reach out before it develops into something even more serious.

Night Eating Syndrome:

The name *night eating syndrome* is fairly self-explanatory, but there are some facets of it that require some further illustration. When an individual has night eating syndrome, they either awaken in the night to engage in eating activities or continue consuming a great deal after dinner time has ended.[3] These behaviors will cause the afflicted person an enormous amount of stress and discomfort, and they will have a full recollection of the behaviors having taken place. This last differs from a disorder where people might eat in their sleep, as with night eating syndrome, the individual is fully aware of what they are doing—they just may have a compulsion to eat throughout the night, or a belief that they will not be able to return to sleep unless they consume a snack.

There are certain risk factors that make someone more likely to develop night eating syndrome, including obesity, anxiety, depression, or even having a different eating disorder.[4] It's thought that the condition likely has something to do with regulating the circadian rhythm and maintaining hormonal balances, though more research is needed to know for sure (as is the case with most eating disorders). If you find yourself compulsively eating at night after dinner and feeling highly distressed as a result, you may have night eating syndrome, and may want to consider seeking help.

Now that we have explored these four subtypes of OSFED, it is time to take a look at some of the physical, emotional, and behavioral signs of the disorder. Keep in mind that many of them will seem remarkably familiar, as there will be a great deal of overlap between the eating disorders we've been introduced already; after all, OSFED touches the edges of anorexia nervosa, bulimia nervosa, and binge eating disorder, so it makes sense that there would be some similarities. Of course, keep in mind that this is by no means meant to be an exhaustive list, and that more information can be found online on the National Eating Disorder Association's website:

Physical Signs:

- Fluctuations in weight, whether it increases or decreases—both can be a red flag. However, it is important to note that in general, the body weight will be in the normal range for height and build.
- Gastrointestinal distress.
- Dizziness and fainting.
- Sleep difficulties, such as insomnia.
- Poor blood work, such as having anemia, deficient hormone levels, slow heart rate in a way that does not imply athleticism, and so on.
- Dental issues, such as cavities from vomiting.
- Yellowing of the skin from eating too many carrots. This may seem like a strange one, but it is actually fairly common among many restrictive eating disorders.
- Slow-healing wounds, particularly on the hands (from vomiting).
- Feeling cold, either internally or to the touch. Sometimes the extremities become cold as the body focuses most of its remaining insulation on the inner organs, and other times it is simply a sensation that the individual reports feeling because their metabolism is slowing down or they are losing weight.
- Thinning of hair on the scalp.
- Dry skin and brittle nails.
- Impaired immune system.

- Cuts, calluses, and scars on the fingers and knuckles as a result of self-induced vomiting (Russell's Sign).[5]

Plainly, there are a variety of physical signs and symptoms that rather run the gamut of eating disorders when it comes to OSFED. All of them are things that we have seen before in other disorders to some degree, with the minor exception of the first: the relatively "normal" body weight. One of the important things to remember about any eating disorder is that the concept of a "normal" body weight is a somewhat antiquated one, and that the only thing that can truly determine whether or not someone is healthy are their vital signs. This is something that is taught exhaustively in eating disorder treatment as a means of helping eating disorder sufferers to recover from poor body image and warped ideals of what it means to be healthy, but it is not brought up in broader society. One might argue that this could contribute, in part, to why eating disorders are becoming increasingly prevalent, but we will delve more into this phenomenon in Chapter Three. For now, it is time to get into what the emotional signs of OSFED can look like. Keep in mind that they will also look quite familiar, as OSFED reaches into the territories of each of the eating disorders we have covered so far.

Emotional Signs:

- Fretting about body shape, body size, and food, though perhaps in a more general way than someone with anorexia nervosa, bulimia nervosa, or binge eating disorder.
- Becoming completely lost in the world of dieting. This can manifest in the form of weighing food, counting calories, trying out multiple fad diets in attempt after attempt to lose more weight, or any other number of ways.
- Developing visible discomfort or expressing discomfort about eating in front of others.
- Withdrawing from usual social circles and becoming unusually quiet, introverted, or even irritable. The last can occur due to hunger; after all, many of us become easily annoyed when we go for too long without food, and those with eating disorders are no exception.

- Experiencing mood swings, more so than the typical ups and downs one might cope with over the course of a day. These are also due to hunger on top of what may already be poor emotional regulation skills.
- May have one or more of the comorbid disorders that were covered in Chapter One: anxiety, depression, OCD, PTSD, and addiction.[6]

The emotional signs and symptoms of OSFED, while quite familiar, are certainly nothing to sneeze at in terms of their potential severity. The emotional aspects of OSFED can be arguably the most painful part of the disorder, as depending on the symptoms that one is suffering from and which subtype they might have, they may be unlikely to die from the disorder on its own . . . but the emotional symptoms can drive eating disorder sufferers to feel completely desperate and alone. OSFED is just as serious as any other eating disorder despite its reputation for being something of a blanket diagnosis for people who have eating disorders that just don't fit into the typical mold of any other condition. It shouldn't be ignored; the behavioral symptoms can be just as disordered as anorexia, bulimia, or binge eating disorder.

Behavioral Signs:

- Dressing in layers to stay warm due to weight loss.
- Dressing in baggy clothes to mask weight loss or to hide perceived flaws.
- Overusing mouthwash, mints, or gum, particularly after meals or snacks. When coupled with frequent trips to the bathroom, this is a red flag for purging through vomiting: the minty fragrance is an attempt to cover up the smell of vomit.
- Developing ritualistic behaviors around eating, such as only eating certain food groups, cutting food into tiny pieces, counting bites before swallowing when eating, and so on.
- Skipping meals or only accepting small portions of food during mealtimes.
- Stealing and stashing food in odd places, such as in bags, furniture, and closets.

- Adopting new diet trends or changing one's diet often with the intent being to lose weight. For instance, someone without an eating disorder might suddenly become a vegetarian after watching a documentary about factory farming, and this would not be indicative of eating disorder behaviors. However, if they suddenly lost interest in animals, restricted their diet to veganism, and expressed interest in losing thirty pounds despite being at a "normal" weight, this would be problematic.
- Denying feeling hungry despite eating very little.
- Complaining of an increasing number of health issues. As we know, the body begins to deteriorate with many eating disorders, and OSFED is no exception to this rule.
- Consuming large quantities of water and other zero-calorie drinks.
- Creating an entirely new life to suit the binge-purge cycle that one may have slipped or be slipping into.[7]

There are many more behavioral signs and symptoms than the ones listed here, but chances are that you are likely already quite well-acquainted with this collection of flags to watch out for, as they have already appeared under the other three eating disorders we have covered thus far. The point is made: OSFED has far-reaching fingers into anorexia, bulimia, and binge eating disorder. It can look like any or all of these conditions, or not quite any of them at all—it is completely dependent on the sufferer. No matter which particular subtype of OSFED someone is struggling with, it is crucial to remember that OSFED is just as serious as any other eating disorder, despite what insurance companies might have you believe. The consequences of having OSFED can be disastrous, whether they are mental, emotional, or physical. It's time to take a look at some of the health consequences that having OSFED can cause, though it is important to keep in mind that the following list is by no means complete due to the far-reaching nature of the disorder.

Health Consequences of OSFED:

- Potential failure of the organs, including the heart, liver, and kidneys.

- Osteoporosis and osteopenia.
- Loss of lean muscle mass.
- Electrolyte imbalances from overconsumption of fluids and purging behaviors.
- General feelings of malaise and fatigue, which can be confusing if the eating disorder sufferer does not realize yet that their behaviors are a problem.
- Gastroparesis, or the slowing of digestion that occurs during starvation behaviors. This can result in severe constipation and abdominal bloating.
- High or low blood pressure.
- Low body temperature.
- High cholesterol.
- Heart disease, if a significant amount of weight is gained due to binging behaviors.
- Type 2 diabetes mellitus (also due to weight gain, as this kind of diabetes is not inheritable).[8]

As always, keep in mind that there are other possible health consequences that may take place when someone is suffering from OSFED, and these are just examples of the negative effects that the disorder can cause. When one sees the health consequences listed out this way, it seems almost ridiculous to suppose that insurance companies would not take OSFED seriously as an eating disorder; it clearly can have very real ramifications on a sufferer's physical well-being. The most important thing to draw away from our conversation about OSFED is that even though it may be an "umbrella diagnosis" for people whose eating disorders don't fit under another category, it must be regarded as just as critically as any other eating disorder.

Now that we have examined OSFED in full, it's time to move onto the next eating disorder on our list: orthorexia nervosa. Orthorexia is sometimes thought to fall underneath the OSFED umbrella, but it deserves its own section in this book because the number of people it is ensnaring is growing and it is increasingly thought to be its own eating disorder, not a subtype.

Orthorexia Nervosa

If you have ever feared for the purity of your food or vowed to only consume products that are organic, you might already be familiar with *orthorexia nervosa* and not even know it. There's nothing wrong with striving to live a healthy, balanced lifestyle, but when that lifestyle turns into a battle just to get through the day, there should be alarm bells ringing in your head for you or your loved one. Orthorexia is more than just a desire to be in shape or generally healthy: it's an overpowering force that drives a person to great lengths to achieve the purest, healthiest form they possibly can, ironically often at the detriment of their actual physical, mental, and spiritual health.

The term *orthorexia nervosa* first appeared in the late '90s to describe the behaviors above, though it has yet to appear in the DSM-5.[9] Therefore, there is some debate in the medical community over whether or not it is a "real" eating disorder, though there are no such doubts shared by those who suffer from it or have close friends, family, or loved ones who have fallen victim to the disorder. It may be difficult to imagine that "eating healthy" could truly present much of an issue, but perhaps it would help to reframe to disorder as more of an obsessive-compulsive condition in which one feels compelled to check labels for forbidden ingredients, denies themselves formerly favorite foods, and exercises to exhaustion in the name of health and purity. Orthorexia may have yet to land itself a firm place in the DSM-5, but it is still a very real eating disorder, despite any medical discourse. Below, we'll list some of the signs and symptoms to look out for if you think you or someone you know could be suffering from orthorexia nervosa.

Physical Signs:

- Some weight loss generally occurs, though how much is extremely dependent on the type of diet the orthorexic individual has deemed the healthiest and purest diet to follow. Sometimes, orthorexic individuals are at a healthy weight for their height and build.
- Fainting and dizzy spells.
- Gastrointestinal distress.
- Impaired immune system.
- Deficiencies in vitamins and minerals as a result of cutting out entire food groups that may have been judged as "unhealthy" or unfit to eat.[10]

In general, those with orthorexia may show any number of physical signs that someone with a more restrictive eating disorder might, as that's what it is: a highly restrictive eating disorder. Only, instead of restricting the quantity of food that is eaten, generally orthorexic individuals will be focused primarily on the types of foods they eat and what goes into them. This can and does cause a great deal of stress for sufferers, and leads to many of the familiar emotional signs and symptoms that we are growing to know quite well by now.

Emotional Signs:

- Worrying about food, ingredients, and origin of food may be the primary concern of someone with orthorexia nervosa. Their distress will come in the form of being healthy and fit, not necessarily being the thinnest they can be. This is one of the places where the disorder differs from anorexia nervosa.
- An overly controlling fascination with what other people are eating.

- Becoming extremely stressed when foods that have been deemed "healthy" are not available. The orthorexic individual may even refuse to eat if said foods are not made available.
- Experiencing one or more of the comorbid disorders that we have covered thus far, particularly OCD, as orthorexia is quite all-consuming in its approach to nutrition and exercise.[11]

Interestingly, orthorexia is not typically as focused on body image as other eating disorders (such as anorexia nervosa and bulimia nervosa) might be, and this shows in the emotional signs and symptoms that may be present in an individual suffering from the condition. They are more likely to have a meltdown over the ingredients on the back of a box of cereal than they are what they see in the mirror, though it's possible—and not entirely uncommon—for orthorexia to develop into anorexia or another eating disorder, as we will observe in Forest's story at the end of the chapter. First, let's explore the behavioral signs of orthorexia.

Behavioral Signs:

- Fervently checking labels of foods in grocery stores to check for specific ingredients that might be deemed "unhealthy" or "impure."
- Exercising excessively in the name of health rather than to achieve thinness.
- Showing high levels of caution or distress when introduced to food that is cooked with ingredients that might not be "safe" or on the list of foods that the orthorexic individual is "allowed" to eat.
- Spending a great deal of time online looking at content that supports healthy eating, exercising, and specific dieting tips that support their "healthy" lifestyle.
- Feeling concerned about the shape or size of one's body may also be a factor, though more often it is a matter of what goes *into* the body that brings about the fear.[12]

There are clear ways in which orthorexia nervosa is a distinct disorder from anorexia nervosa, though they do share some commonalities in the health effects arena. Orthorexia is a restrictive disorder just as much as it is an obsessive one, and it has many of the same potential deleterious health problems as anorexia or any other restrictive eating disorder.

Health Consequences of Orthorexia Nervosa:

- Osteoporosis and osteopenia.
- Malnutrition, which may seem odd—after all, orthorexic individuals have a fixation on eating "healthy." However, in truth, they are cutting out many essential food groups and are drastically narrowing their diets.
- Lowered body temperature.
- Poor immune system function.
- Possible infertility, which can be heartbreaking for those who intend to start families. This typically can be reversed once the body heals, as long as the individual with the eating disorder stays dedicated to their recovery.
- Thinning of the hair on the scalp and growth of lanugo on other parts of the body.
- Organ failure, including the heart, kidneys, and liver.
- Issues with thinking clearly and emotional regulation. This is typical with any starvation diet, and can occur in people that don't even have eating disorders if they are starving or not receiving the nutrition they need.[13]

As with any eating disorder, there are consequences that go beyond those that take place inside the body. Orthorexia can be extremely isolating; when someone is spending all of their time worrying about their food and the ingredients that it is composed of, it can suck the joy out of family meals, going out with friends, and trying any new food spontaneously. When someone has orthorexia, they truly believe that what they are doing is the righteous, healthy thing, but in reality they are greatly damaging both their physical and mental well-being. It is perhaps the most bitter demonstration of irony that a disorder that demands health above all else comes at such a terrible cost.

It's time to explore another eating disorder that you may not have heard of: *ARFID*, or *Avoidant Restrictive Feeding or Intake Disorder*. ARFID presents quite differently from the eating disorders we have examined so far, so if you feel that you struggle with an eating disorder and haven't found one that describes your behaviors yet, this one may be it.

ARFID

ARFID can be mistaken for anorexia nervosa or another restrictive eating disorder if one is not carefully observing the behaviors of the afflicted individual. Like anorexia, bulimia, OSFED, and orthorexia, someone with ARFID will have fear foods, but the motivation behind having the fear foods will be different than someone with any of these other eating disorders. Someone with anorexia might fear a food because of the calories within it. A person with bulimia might fear a food because of their tendency to binge on it. But a person with ARFID may be frightened of foods because they worry they may choke, become sick, or simply not enjoy eating them.

It may help to think of ARFID as the "picky eating" eating disorder. It can be particularly prevalent in children, and can, at first, be mistaken for just that—extremely picky eating. However, ARFID goes beyond the ordinary likes and dislikes that someone might have of tastes, textures, and temperatures of foods, and it becomes restrictive and limiting in life, causing weight loss and sometimes even malnutrition. Like orthorexia, it can be isolating, but unlike orthorexia, it is in the DSM-5. Let's take a look at the DSM-5 criteria now:

1. An eating or feeding disturbance (e.g., apparent lack of interest in eating or food; avoidance based on the sensory characteristics of food; concern about aversive consequences of eating) as manifested by persistent failure to meet appropriate nutritional and/or energy needs associated with one (or more) of the following:

> Significant weight loss (or failure to achieve expected weight gain or faltering growth in children).
>
> Significant nutritional deficiency.
>
> Dependence on enteral feeding or oral nutritional supplements.
>
> Marked interference with psychosocial functioning.

2. The disturbance is not better explained by lack of available food or by an associated culturally sanctioned practice.

3. The eating disturbance does not occur exclusively during the course of anorexia nervosa or bulimia nervosa, and there is no evidence of a disturbance in the way in which one's body weight or shape is experienced.

4. The eating disturbance is not attributable to a concurrent medical condition or not better explained by another mental disorder. When the eating disturbance occurs in the context of another condition or disorder, the severity of the eating disturbance exceeds that routinely associated with the condition or disorder and warrants additional clinical attention.[14]

It is quite plain to see that ARFID is its own, distinctive eating disorder in the same way that the other disorders we have discussed are (except, one could argue, for OSFED, as it touches on a wide variety of conditions.) In addition to these specifications from the DSM-5, there are also three subtypes of ARFID that one may have:

1. Lack of Interest: People with this type of ARFID genuinely lack interest in eating and food as a concept. They also tend to get full quickly, so eating "normal" amounts may be uncomfortable for them.

2. Sensory Avoidance: Those with this subtype fear foods that conjure specific sensory experiences. They may not like foods that are mushy, or too warm, or too cold, or too chewy, or smell like cinnamon, or any number of other sensory events that could trigger a negative reaction in the individual. People on the autism spectrum are more likely to have this subtype of ARFID than those who are not.

3. Fear of Negative Consequences: Finally, someone with this subtype of ARFID may fear choking, food allergies, nausea after eating, or other adverse consequences from eating. These fears are debilitating, and interfere with the afflicted person's ability to eat in a normalized fashion.[15]

No matter which form of ARFID you find yourself or someone close to you struggling with, each one can be physically, mentally, and socially devastating, and it's important to catch it early. If it gets out of hand, it can lead to the same negative health effects as any other restrictive eating disorder. However, it can add a layer of danger if one develops the disorder in childhood, as proper nutrition is necessary to grow and nourish the body as it does so. Some of the physical signs and symptoms of ARFID can look quite a bit like anorexia nervosa, and thus will look very familiar to you when we list them out below:

Physical Signs:

- Dizziness and fainting.
- Thinning of the hair on the head and growth of lanugo on the body.
- Dry skin.
- Brittle nails.
- Poor lab work showing anemia, low potassium, hormone imbalances, and the like.
- Nonspecific gastrointestinal distress.
- Menstrual cycle irregularities and eventual infertility in some cases.
- Cognitive issues, such as trouble concentrating.

- Insomnia.[16]

As promised, these physical signs rather resemble those that we have seen in several other eating disorders. As always, it is vital to keep in mind that ARFID is its own condition and should not be considered to be less serious simply because the physical symptoms are something we have seen before. However, something that *will* look a little different are the emotional signs of ARFID.

Emotional Signs:

- Unlike in cases of anorexia, bulimia, and other similar eating disorders, there is no desire to lose weight involved with ARFID. This is a very important distinction to make when it comes to determining if an eating disorder could be ARFID or another disorder.
- Fear of choking, disliking, or becoming ill from certain foods, or from many foods.
- Becoming stressed or even frightened when presented with new foods.
- Developing one or more of the comorbid disorders that we learned about in Chapter One. However, people with ARFID are most likely to be autistic, have ADHD, or have anxiety as well.[17, 18]

As we learned in the opening of this section, the motivations for ARFID are different than for other eating disorders, so it makes sense that the emotional signs and symptoms for the condition would present a little dissimilarly to other disorders. It plainly is a highly anxious eating disorder, as it is often anxiety over particular food attributes that drives the condition to manifest in the first place. It is not uncommon for people suffering from ARFID to have specific behaviors that set them apart from other types of eating disorders as well.

Behavioral Signs:

- Dressing in layers to stay warm.

- Losing a significant amount of weight as a result of feeling increasingly uncomfortable ingesting foods.
- Only eating foods of specific textures, such as soft foods, as they may be less likely to cause choking than a rough or crunchy food, for example.
- Limiting foods to only a select few that may become fewer as the disorder progresses.
- Seeming to truly lack appetite or interest in food as a whole.
- Starting to restrict food groups or certain types of foods that one might eat, such as vegetables. This kind of restriction will not have to do with calories or a desire to lose weight.
- Complaining about gastrointestinal issues, such as stomach pains or constipation.[19]

There are some ways in which ARFID may misrepresent itself as anorexia nervosa, as you can see in some of the behaviors: dressing in layers and avoiding entire food groups could easily be mistaken for anorexia and not seen for what it is. It is crucial to look out for the other signs and symptoms of ARFID, particularly in picky children, lest it be missed or mistaken for an entirely different eating disorder despite there being no body image issues present whatsoever. Next, it's time to look over some of the health consequences of ARFID, of which there can be quite a few.

Health Consequences of ARFID:

- Possible and probable malnutrition as a result of cutting out specific foods or entire food groups that are deemed "unsafe" to consume.
- Weight loss due to unintentional restriction.
- In children, failure to gain healthy weight appropriate for one's height and build—the kind of weight that one needs to grow properly.
- Dry hair and brittle nails from lack of nutrition.
- Thinning of hair on head with growth of lanugo on the body.
- Developmental delays.
- Gastrointestinal problems (stomach aches, acid reflux).

- Poor immune system function and slow-healing wounds.[20]

Many of the health consequences of ARFID can be identical to that of anorexia nervosa if the onset of anorexia is early enough (childhood). ARFID is easy to push away as simply picky eating that will go away on its own over time, and in many cases, it will not without the proper treatment and help. There is more to ARFID than meets the eye, and it goes beyond casual likes or dislikes at the dinner table. ARFID is a well-documented disorder, and though it is relatively new to the DSM-5, it is not new to those who suffer from it.[21]

Now that we have fully explored ARFID in detail, it's time to jump into our next eating disorder: pica. *Pica* may seem especially outlandish, but try to keep in mind that an eating disorder is an eating disorder, and that no matter how unusual or strange the behaviors of the condition may seem to us, they are still quite real and difficult to cope with. So, without further delay, let's get to discussing pica and its various characteristics, DSM-5 classification, and signs and symptoms.

Pica

If you feel strong cravings (or notice someone else in your life, especially someone who is young or developmentally disabled) to eat non-food items, you may be suffering from a disorder called pica. The non-food items typically take the form of clay, paint chips, dirt, and other potentially dangerous substances that ought not to be ingested in any quantity.[22] If you do not have pica, your first question may be why, when it comes to the reason behind someone's drive to swallow paint or even hair, but there are a few theories that may explain the motivation behind the eating disorder. It is widely accepted in the medical community that if someone has pica, they must be eating the non-food items in an attempt to gain nutrition where they are not getting it elsewhere in their diets. In uncommon cases, pregnant women develop the disorder, usually eating dirt, and it is believed that this is due to an iron or zinc deficiency.[23] Whatever the case, pica did make it into the DSM-5, though the criteria is rather short and unhelpful for someone who may be reading it to determine if they have illness:

1. There are no laboratory tests for pica. Instead, the diagnosis is made from a clinical history of the patient.
2. Diagnosing pica should be accompanied by tests for anemia, potential intestinal blockages, and toxic side effects of substances consumed (i.e., lead in paint, bacteria, or parasites in dirt).[24]

Not only can pica be a little unusual to read about, but it can be quite dangerous. It can cause a variety of physical complications that make it a hazardous disorder to bear. For instance, someone who is picking off and ingesting the paint on their living room wall may not realize that it is lead-based, thus leading to lead poisoning. Or someone who is eating too much clay or other similar substances can wind up with blockages in their bowels. Any number of things can show up in a person that might indicate they are struggling with pica.

Physical Signs:

- Stomach and gastrointestinal issues, such as stomach aches and pains.
- Bloody stool.
- Constipation and/or diarrhea.
- Blockages in the bowels from eating solid objects or objects that can seal the bowels once swallowed.
- Infections.
- Dental issues from eating hard objects like rocks.[25]

Pica is primarily an invisible disease, as it is not an eating disorder that is focused in any way on weight loss or changing body shape or size. It is often present in people with co-occurring disorders, including disorders that we have not discussed within this book, such as excoriation disorder (or skin picking disorder), trichotillomania (hair pulling disorder), and in those with developmental disabilities, as we mentioned in the opening paragraph of this module.[26] Because pica is not generally an emotionally driven illness, we will be skipping the emotional signs section and moving right along to the behavioral signs and symptoms to watch for if you are worried that you or someone you know could be developing pica.

Behavioral Signs:

- Eating non-food materials, such as the ones that we covered above (paint chips, dirt, clay, hair, and so on).
- Ingesting non-food items that are *not* part of a cultural practice of any sort.
- Feeling open, by and large, to eating actual foods.
- Consuming different non-food items based on availability. Additionally, the types of materials eaten may change as the individual ages.[27]

It is important to note here that there is something of an age range in which an individual may be diagnosed with pica. After all, mouthing behaviors are normal in infants and babies, and occasionally ingestion does happen, but this does not qualify as an eating disorder behavior.[28] Moreover, it is highly unusual for eating disorders to present in infants at all, even an eating disorder like pica (or ARFID, for that matter, though these would be more likely out of those we've presented so far). The point is that pica is not meant to be a diagnosis for people who simply like to put things in their mouths, as babies do. It can be quite dangerous and lead to adverse health consequences.

Health Consequences of Pica:

- Potential for poisoning due to eating non-food items with high levels of toxicity.
- A *bezoar*, or a mass of material that cannot be digested, may become present in the stomach or intestines.
- Infections.

Pica is not likely to cause death, but it can cause illness or be indicative of malnutrition all on its own, thus causing the disorder to continue if neither condition is properly treated. Those with pica don't typically fall into the same pit of despair as those with other eating disorders might, though it would still be understandable to see how someone with pica might grow to feel secretive or ashamed of their eating behaviors if they carried on into adulthood or worsened with time. Just like any other eating disorder, those with pica need to be met with care and understanding so that they might hope to recover from the disorder. Most of the time, pica can be cured with vitamin and mineral supplementation, but when it is due to something else (as might be the case in a comorbid disorder), there are other treatment options available that will be explored in more depth in Chapter Four.

For now, it's time to take a look at the next eating disorder on our list: diabulimia. *Diabulimia* may be up there with anorexia in terms of its potential lethality, but it's still a mental illness that is fairly shrouded in mystery. Chances are that you hadn't heard of it before we just introduced its name, but that isn't your fault. None of the eating disorders in this chapter receive the same attention as the three in the previous chapter, which is why this chapter exists. Now, let's turn to diabulimia and learn about what diabetes mellitus and eating disorders can have in common.

Diabulimia

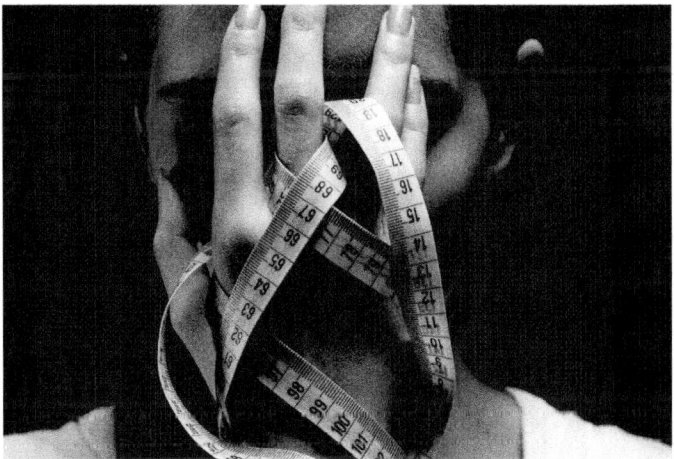

Depending on who you are, diabulimia—also in the medical community by the name "ED-DMT1"—may be the deadliest eating disorder you have never heard of. That may sound like a dramatization, but diabulimia sets the perfect snare for predisposed individuals who already have one extra medical strike against them to fall into: diabetes mellitus. Diabulimia is more likely to affect those with Type 1 diabetes than Type 2, but either type can develop this eating disorder that is reserved exclusively for those who have comorbid diabetes, too.

What is diabulimia, and why does only such a specific subset of the population get it? Diabulimia is a vicious disorder that, like orthorexia, does not yet have its own place in the DSM-5. Instead, it falls in between anorexia nervosa and bulimia nervosa, though which one it more closely resembles depends on which behaviors are the most prominent in the individual with the eating disorder. The way diabulimia works is that the afflicted person will manipulate their insulin levels in order to lose weight. According to the National Eating Disorder Association, this is considered a purging behavior, as it is a means of getting rid of one's food after consumption. It is also possible for diabulimia to simply be classified as OSFED.[28]

There are a number of physical signs and symptoms that occur with diabulimia that can tip you off that someone in your life may be struggling with the disorder. Some of them may be difficult to notice unless you are closely monitoring the diabetes maintenance of your loved one, but others will be more plain to see. Examples of these symptoms are as follows:

Physical Symptoms:

- Abrupt or unexplained weight loss. This on its own is not necessarily enough to suspect diabulimia, but if you notice it in addition to the other signs on these lists, make sure to take note.
- Frequent nausea and vomiting episodes.
- Frequent urination/trips to the bathroom. This will go hand in hand with being constantly thirsty and drinking lots of water.
- Fatigue that begins to set in as the body deteriorates and blood sugar fluctuates.
- Increasingly poor vision, which is a side effect that occurs when diabetes is not being properly taken care of.
- Lack of menstruation.
- Low sodium and perhaps low potassium as well, both of which can be very harmful and even deadly if left unchecked or allowed to pass certain thresholds.

- A1c is 9.0 or higher regularly, which is dangerous and increases the risk for damage to the eyes, kidneys, and more.
- A1c levels don't match the meter level readings.
- Begins to experience an unusual number of DKA (Diabetic Ketoacidosis) episodes.[29]

As promised, some of these signs are easier to notice than others, but one thing is for certain: all of them are equally as dangerous. Diabulimia is disastrous to one's health . . . but we're getting ahead of ourselves. The disorder is also highly distressing for those who suffer from it, and brings forth a variety of emotional signs and symptoms.

Emotional Signs:

- Becoming careless or unforthcoming about diabetes care and management, especially if it is a new behavior.
- Developing an irrational worry that insulin makes one "fat."
- Anxiety directed toward body shape and size, as well as diet.
- Fearing blood sugar that falls below desired numbers, generally numbers that are very high (as higher numbers are more likely to cause involuntary weight loss).
- Feeling uncomfortable injecting insulin and testing blood sugars in front of other people. This could be easily mistaken as shyness about having diabetes, but in individuals with diabulimia, they may want to avoid injecting appropriate amounts of insulin and making their A1c levels known.
- Becoming increasingly withdrawn from friends, family, and social circles.
- Struggling with one or more comorbid disorders, particularly anxiety or depression.[30]

Some of these signs may have looked similar to other eating disorders, such as anorexia or bulimia, which would make sense: it is, after all, sometimes considered to be an offshoot of one of these disorders. However, some of the emotional signs are quite specific to diabulimia, such as anything that has to do with fussing with one's A1c levels. It is clearly a unique and powerful condition, despite not receiving its own classification within the DSM-5, and the behavioral signs that one presents when they are struggling with the disorder are just as debilitating as the emotional signs and symptoms.

Behavioral Signs:

- Eating much more or quite a bit less than usual.
- Only eating certain foods or food groups so that one may only have to inject as little amount of insulin as possible to get by. Certain foods demand more insulin than others, so those with diabulimia may restrict their food choices in order to accommodate this.
- Eating only in private.
- Coming up with new, strict food rules.
- Forming a strict workout regimen.
- Sleeping more often.
- Increasingly inconsistent with filling prescription medications (as they relate to diabetes).[31]

An important detail here to mention when it comes to diabulimia is the fact that the cause of the condition can be a little different than that of other eating disorders (though not necessarily). Sometimes it has to do with a fear of gaining weight or concerns about how one looks and feels in one's body, and other times it may have to do with a phenomenon known as diabetes burnout.[32] *Diabetes burnout* refers to a state in which a person with diabetes begins to feel exhausted by the process of caring for the disease, and they may begin to completely neglect their blood sugar levels, which can be very dangerous. Whatever the case is for the cause of diabulimia, the end result may be the same: a wide array of health consequences that can even be lethal if left untreated.

Health Consequences of Diabulimia:

- Diabetic Ketoacidosis.
- Slow wound healing.
- Staph infections and other infections as a result of having chronically high blood sugar.

- Yeast infections.
- Muscle atrophy. When the body does not have enough insulin, it cannot make use of food and begins to starve, which is what causes weight loss in the first place.[33]
- Dehydration, often severe, due to the body's attempts to expel the excess ketones that starvation has created within it.[34]
- Electrolyte imbalances, which, as we know, can be extremely dangerous and possibly fatal if left unchecked.
- Retinopathy, which can lead to eventual blindness if it is not properly treated.
- Peripheral Neuropathy, a painful condition that affects the extremities.
- Organ damage to the kidneys, heart, and liver.
- Potential for coma or stroke.[35]

There are plenty more health consequences that may possibly appear as a result of having diabulimia, either in the short or long term, but these are simply meant to act as examples to illustrate just what limiting one's insulin can do to the body. It certainly doesn't help that diabulimia is so unknown, as it means that people are unlikely to recognize the signs and may not catch the disorder until it is too far along. If you or someone you know is suffering from symptoms of diabulimia, be sure to seek help right away, just as you would with any other eating disorder. It is no less serious or deadly than the other eating disorders we've mentioned thus far.

Our next eating disorder does happen to be in the DSM-5, but it is more similar to pica than any of the other eating disorders we have studied so far. Rumination disorder is our next and final eating disorder before we meet Forest, an eating disorder survivor, who—like Heidi—is discovering the road to recovery in his own way.

Rumination Disorder

Rumination disorder may be the least like the other eating disorders we have looked at, in that it typically involves no emotional distress whatsoever, apart from perhaps some embarrassment during or after the act. When someone has rumination disorder, they repeatedly regurgitate their food after eating involuntarily—not to be confused with purging. It happens so soon after eating that the food is chewable and may be swallowed again or spat out, but it is not acidic like vomit.[36] In order to be diagnosed with rumination disorder, one must display the following characteristics, according to the DSM-5:

1. Repeated regurgitation of food for a period of at least one month. Regurgitated food may be re-chewed, re-swallowed, or spit out.
2. The repeated regurgitation is not due to a medication condition (e.g., gastrointestinal condition).
3. The behavior does not occur exclusively in the course of anorexia nervosa, bulimia nervosa, BED, or avoidant/restrictive food intake disorder.
4. If occurring in the presence of another mental disorder (e.g., intellectual developmental disorder), it is severe enough to warrant independent clinical attention.[37]

Notably, there are no body image disturbances present with rumination disorder, and it does not involve any overexercising, restrictive behaviors, binging behaviors, or any attempts to control weight. In fact, it has nothing to do with weight or body image at all. The most distressing part of rumination disorder are the potential physical and health effects, as a person with the condition may not be particularly troubled by it beyond the inconvenience of the repeated regurgitation. Physical signs of the disorder may be fairly obvious, but there are a few that, after listing out, will prompt brief discussion.

Physical Signs:

- Repeated regurgitation of food. This regurgitation will be easy and will generally happen within ten minutes after eating.
- Bad breath.
- Feeling full.
- Pressure in the abdominal region that is ultimately relieved by regurgitation.
- Nausea and feeling sick to the stomach.

- Unintentional weight loss, if one is spitting out the regurgitated food rather than chewing and swallowing it again.[38]

It is the pressure that occurs in the abdominal region that the medical community believes is the cause for rumination disorder, though the exact causes of the disorder are still a mystery. Regardless, the disorder can still cause some medical complications, even though it typically is not related directly to any emotional turmoil like other eating disorders are (though it is more likely to occur in people who have existing psychiatric conditions like anxiety and depression).[39] Because there are no particular emotional symptoms to look out for when paying attention to rumination disorder, and it is not a disorder that focuses much on specific eating disorder behaviors, we will be skipping directly to the health consequences section.

Health Consequences of Rumination Disorder:

- Erosion of the teeth.
- Malnutrition.
- Weight loss.
- Esophageal damage.[40]

As was mentioned previously (albeit briefly), rumination disorder can also be quite isolating and embarrassing. If you are always accidentally regurgitating your food, it can make it difficult to socialize at mealtimes, go out with friends, or enjoy spontaneous activities that involve eating. As always, the emotional damage of having an eating disorder, even one that has the potential to have a minimal emotional impact like rumination disorder, cannot be underestimated.

We've officially toured each of the major well-known and lesser-known eating disorders and their subtypes. There is a good chance that some of these eating disorders—if not most—were new to you, simply because they are not well publicized and do not receive the public awareness that they deserve. Eating disorders in general, perhaps, are not given enough attention (as we will explore in the next chapter), but the ones we covered here are particularly shrouded in mystery. With luck, you now understand a little better your own struggles with an eating disorder, or those of someone you are close to. If you still need guidance, that's perfectly alright: next up, we will meet Forest, an individual who, like Heidi from the previous chapter, has offered to share his story with you. Perhaps his words can help to provide some insight.

Forest's Story

Forest wrestles with a hodgepodge of diagnoses, though he's never been quite sure what his own eating disorder diagnosis looks like on paper. While some eating disorder sufferers' conditions remain more or less constant in terms of how they present, Forest's disorder has been more like a chameleon. It started in his youth, and he can recall his earliest symptoms dating back to a conversation his parents had in the car when he was five. He was in the car on the way home from church or a violin lesson, and they had gotten fast-food as a treat. His parents jokingly mentioned how the french fries they were enjoying were going to give them heart disease, and though as an adult, Forest knows they meant nothing by the comment, as a child, Forest found himself abruptly petrified of french fries. After that, he restricted himself to one french fry a year in hopes of saving his heart, which was perhaps an abnormal worry for a five-year-old to have. This was only the beginning of what would snowball into a much more serious struggle with a full-blown eating disorder . . . but that wouldn't come until much later.

Forest describes his childhood as unremarkable. He experienced no obvious trauma apart from some mild bullying, came from a loving, body-positive household that preached an "everything in moderation" approach to food, and had access to virtually everything he could want in terms of activities. He was well-liked in his small, rural elementary and middle school, and generally felt good in his skin, though he does remember becoming aware of his body and a desire to be the thinnest person among his friends at around the time puberty hit. All of this is to say that, to Forest, the cause of his eating disorder is more or less a mystery to him. In his own words, "Sometimes I think that I was just destined to have one, and that this is my struggle to contend with."

However, in the eighth grade, things started to sour a little for Forest. In addition to having an eating disorder, Forest has several other co-occurring diagnoses, including the bipolar subtype of schizoaffective disorder. It was at this point in his life that he recalls having his first schizophrenic delusions, and though he expressed them in passing to a few friends and they caused him some stress, they wound up resolving on their own and he entered high school without incident. His eating disorder, along with his schizophrenia and mood disorder, lurked beneath the surface of his mind for the time being, and did not fully emerge again until his sophomore year.

Forest experienced his first bipolar depression in the tenth grade, and with it emerged a whole host of unhealthy coping skills, including the start of his eating disorder. He ate the exact same thing for lunch every day, restricting if he could, and stopped having his lunch in front of his friends at school. Instead, he ate in a bathroom stall in secret, reading the same book over and over in an attempt to save himself from the pit he could feel himself teetering on the edge of. It was a miserable way to live, and as he lost weight, he grew more miserable. He was visited by suicidal thoughts and urges. During this time in his life, which lasted roughly six months, he also began self-harming for the first time, which would haunt him for many years afterwards. As many people with eating disorders do, he experienced disruptions in his sleep, and found himself lying awake for hours in bed, listening to the classical music station on the radio. When his mood finally shifted and he was freed from the grips of his depression, he was cautiously optimistic that things would be okay, and they were. At least, for a while.

As Forest describes it, the rest of high school was a blur of delusions, hallucinations, and highs and lows. As schizophrenia and bipolar disorder began to truly set in—as well as an increasingly tumultuous family life at home with his parents divorcing—Forest's life began to change drastically. He believes that if anything, this may have been the catalyst to what really started his eating disorder, which began to take off his junior year of high school. For no particular reason that he can figure, Forest became possessed with a desire to lose weight and eat healthier. He decided that he was going to force himself to like certain foods that he had previously disliked as long as they were healthy, eat smaller lunches, and get more exercise. He began riding his bike to and from school everyday, as well as taking long rides into the desert areas around his home to get in better shape. He started counting calories, watching documentaries about health and fitness, and read article after article online about food. There was nothing he would not learn in his free time, and he began to develop a reputation among his friends as the "healthy one." He took pride in this, and it felt like he was doing the right thing. In truth, Forest was beginning to fall into the hands of orthorexia, but he wouldn't come to this realization until later.

Finally, high school graduation came, and Forest went off to the University of California, Santa Cruz. He relates his time there as a collage of moderate successes and enormous failures, as he has had to return and drop out more times than he can count due to mental health issues. He did not adjust well to his first several weeks at university, and was so anxious that he barely left his room. He lived in an apartment with six other people, and he was such a recluse that they didn't even know his name. He didn't eat much, but he did find his way to the gym on campus, and his eating disorder—if it hadn't already been there—exploded into a fully fledged eating disorder for the first time.

It may have been mania that caused Forest to push himself to his limits initially, but he quickly grew addicted to the sensation of running on a treadmill. One of his medications caused him to have a manic episode that resulted in him sometimes running ten miles a day on no sleep and feeling on top of the world afterwards. It never occurred to him that what he was doing was harmful or unsustainable, but he did wind up injuring his foot during one of his runs. It turned out to only be inflammation and he was told to rest, but Forest simply took the medication he was prescribed and kept running because he couldn't fathom the idea of stopping and feared that he might gain weight if he did.

After a time, Forest crashed from his manic high, but he didn't stop working out obsessively. His fear of gaining weight grew, and the food on his plate shrank. His concern with being healthy started to take a backseat to his desire to be thin. His workouts got longer and harder, but his body stopped cooperating. He started to feel so exhausted after each workout that he could barely walk or ride his bike home afterward. Not knowing what else to do, he went to UCSC's student health center and discovered that his blood pressure and body temperature were quite low, but no one seemed concerned, so he left without answers.

Life went on like this for a long, long time. Forest's health continued to deteriorate, but his eating disorder made him believe that if only he worked harder, he would achieve the body that he dreamed of, and his energy level would return with it. He was, of course, wrong: his body was beginning to shut down, and he didn't know it.

Everything came to a head one day when Forest broke down while trying to count the calories in a single blueberry. He realized that what he was doing to himself was a problem, to say the least, and he knew that he needed help if he was going to recover. Knowing that his moment of clarity wouldn't last, he called his mom, and though she was dismayed and confused to hear about how he was treating his body, she listened and agreed to get him the help he needed. He went to the first of what would become several treatment centers over the years, and though it helped him, Forest describes himself as not quite ready to give up his eating disorder at that period even though he was the one who reached out for help. He exercised in secret, self-harmed, and occasionally even drank. Overall, however, when he left the treatment center, he was in better shape than when he had arrived.

The next half-decade of Forest's life was much of the same. His mental health landed him in psychiatric wards in hospitals far away from home repeatedly, and his eating disorder continued to ebb and flow. As he grew older, his eating disorder behaviors began to transform from orthorexia and atypical anorexia to something more closely-resembling OSFED. He began to purge his food through vomiting, though any binges that followed the resulting starvation cycle were rare and quite small. This behavior began to get out of control while in a treatment facility that did not treat eating disorders, so he was sent to a residential treatment center to recuperate from his eating disorder in late 2020, this time determined to recover for good.

While in treatment, Forest finally took advantage of the skill sets that he had been taught over the years for managing his emotions and eating disorder urges by sharing how he was feeling in group and individual therapy, utilizing dialectical behavior therapy skills (we will explore what this means in Chapter Five), and taking advantage of the time away from home to do some soul-searching. He rediscovered what his dreams were, and dedicated himself to pursuing them. He even considered going back to school once he was finished with treatment, though he admits that that particular dream wound up not panning out, which he is completely okay with.

Present-day Forest lives back home with his mother and stepfather in the town he grew up in, but he's preparing to move out soon. He works two jobs that he loves, is in a healthy, supportive relationship, and maintains a great deal of friendships that he holds dear to his heart. His mental health and eating disorder have been stable since his last round in treatment ended in the spring of 2021, which he considers to be his own version of a success story. He has been at a healthy weight for the duration of this time and thinks very little about losing weight or dieting, and finds meaning in other areas of his life now where he couldn't before.

Forest's story demonstrates that eating disorders can come in a variety of shapes and sizes, and that sometimes the causes behind eating disorders either aren't clear because of the disorders that occur alongside them. When someone like Forest is struggling with a variety of mental health disorders in addition to an eating disorder, they can not only exacerbate the condition, but can lead to it in the first place. If you or someone you know is wrestling with depression, psychosis, anxiety, or another malady while having an eating disorder, you know exactly how impossible it can make handling the trials and tribulations of everyday life seem. Sometimes, it can feel as though there is no way out, and during times like those, you may need to reach out for support. However, not everyone is fortunate enough to have people in their lives who they can talk to when they are feeling so terribly low, so sometimes there has to be an alternative. In Chapter One, we provided you with the option to text Crisis Text

Line, but if you don't have access to a cell phone, that won't be very handy. The National Suicide Prevention Lifeline is available at 800-273-8255, with help on hand in both English and Spanish. If you can't text, you can pick up a phone and call at any time of the day or night to talk.

If you need help, ask for it. You'll be glad you did.

THREE

Eating Disorder Causes

THE CURIOUS THING about eating disorders is that, at the end of the day, no one is quite certain what causes them. There are many theories—several of which are well established and are what we will be focusing on primarily within this chapter—but the truth behind what causes someone to starve themselves or eat until they can no longer move is lacking data to back up the facts. Eating disorders are cunning, insidious, and mysterious diseases of the mind that can creep in and take hold of nearly anyone . . . but what are the risk factors? Can eating disorders be prevented, or if you have these risk factors, is it game over? What about a particular person or environment can make someone more susceptible to developing an eating disorder, if such things factor in? All of these questions and more will be answered within this chapter as we explore what is known about the causes of eating disorders.

We touched upon it all the way back in the beginning of Chapter One, but there are several elements that go into making an eating disorder an eating disorder. As a refresher, these elements are genetic, biological, psychological, and sociocultural. Although much more research is needed to know for certain how each of these pieces of the puzzle fit into the whole of an eating disorder, we will be discussing what we do know in detail about each of them, below.

Genetic Factors

While there is no concrete evidence yet to suggest that eating disorders are absolutely heritable, there is some compelling support for the notion that if someone in an individual's family has had an eating disorder, it puts other susceptible individuals at an increased risk for developing one, too. This is due to the way the body works, not the scary notion that eating disorders can be passed down from one person to another. For instance, in people who have eating disorders, it has been discovered that chemicals in the brain that control digestion, hunger, and appetite are no longer in balance.[1] However, that isn't to say that there isn't some likelihood for heritability to be involved if an individual is born into a family in which there have been high rates of eating disorders. In fact, those with a family member who has an eating disorder are 7–12 times more likely to develop an eating disorder themselves.[2]

Furthermore, eating disorder personality traits may be inheritable as well, which may be in part why eating disorders show up in the first place. Many people who suffer from eating disorders tend to have a specific set of characteristics in common, including:

- Perfectionism.
- Anxious personalities.
- Obsessive personalities.
- Rigidity.
- Being hypersensitive toward reward and punishment.
- Impulsivity.

As always, it is important to keep in mind that this list is not meant to describe each person with an eating disorder or to stereotype; it is simply there to illustrate that there seem to be commonalities between eating disorder sufferers, particularly those suffering from anorexia nervosa, bulimia nervosa, and directly related disorders. Of course, this discussion could easily turn to one of nature versus nurture: are you born with your personality traits, or are they programmed into you by your environment and the people you are exposed to? We will get further into that in later sections, but for now, let's examine one last topic before we move forward: chromosomes.

In 1996, an organization known as the Price Foundation began to explore exactly what makes eating disorders occur, specifically anorexia and bulimia. What they found was incredible. After compiling an enormous amount of data over the course of several years, they unearthed a few areas on chromosomes 1 and 10 that wound up looking like areas for anorexia and bulimia to lurk.[3] Although it looks unpromising that there will be a single gene that will prove responsible for eating disorders (which would be very convenient for future medical procedures that might be able to "heal" the gene once the abnormality is spotted), studies like these are still ongoing and are making huge strides toward getting to the bottom of the genetic side of mental illnesses like eating disorders.

Before we move on, it is important to remember that none of this information is meant to frighten, especially if you have family members who have had or do have eating disorders. This does not necessarily mean that you are doomed to develop one yourself. It only means that, since genes play a role in the development of eating disorders, you may be at a higher risk for developing an eating disorder than someone who does not have the same genes as you. If you do not have an eating disorder and are reading this book for a loved one who does, keep this in mind and take care of yourself, making sure that you approach how you treat yourself with love and compassion. Even if you weren't at a slightly elevated risk, you would deserve it.

Biological Factors

We touched upon it in our last section about genetics, but there are a handful of biological causes that are theorized to be behind eating disorders. Some of them, as we have covered, occur on a chromosomal level, but others have to do with neurotransmitters in the brain. Neurotransmitters are chemicals that communicate messages to the various parts of the brain and central nervous system.[4] There are many different kinds of neurotransmitters, and several are thought to have to do with eating disorders, including one called serotonin. Serotonin has an effect on the appetite, and can help us determine whether or not we are full after meals. It also has an emotional effect, controlling emotional responses and judgement.[5] All of these factors are impaired in people who suffer from eating disorders, particularly those who binge.

Additionally, abnormalities have been observed in the structure of the brain in those who have eating disorders. The hypothalamus, a structure that is accountable for a great deal of functions, including regulating eating and fullness, does not quite function correctly in a person who has, say, bulimia nervosa.[6] When someone has bulimia, their brain may be telling them to eat beyond ordinary levels of satiation, or even telling them that they do not feel full in the first place, thus being more likely to prompt a binge.

As is typically the case with eating disorders, many more studies are needed to fully reveal the many potential biological causes that may be hiding underneath the surface of what we currently know about eating disorders. There are likely a multitude of biological factors that play into making an eating disorder an eating disorder, but it's also important to remember that these are not *just* biological and genetic diseases; there are several other elements that are theorized to cause eating disorders. Next, we will be diving into the psychological factors behind the conditions, of which there are many.

Psychological Factors

Psychology and psychiatry are undoubtedly complex subjects, and this is no exception. As we covered in Chapter One, there is no shortage of comorbid disorders that can come along with eating disorders, including (but not limited to): anxiety, depression, OCD, and PTSD. This last disorder is quite common among eating disorder sufferers, as childhood sexual abuse seems to spur trauma that manifests as eating disorders later in life.[7] Of course, not everyone who has an eating disorder suffered childhood sexual trauma or has trauma at all, but having trauma of some sort seems to be a common denominator when it comes to eating disorders. Whether that trauma comes in the form of bullying (online or in person), neglect, abuse, or another source, it still seems to be a contributor to these conditions. After all, if we look at the personal account of Heidi from earlier in this book and use her as an example, her trauma of being friendless and bullied left an opening for an eating disorder to sneak in and take hold. Not everyone's story is the same, and, as previously mentioned, not everyone with an eating disorder has trauma to speak of . . . but it is certainly worth noting as a psychological element.

Another psychological risk factor for developing an eating disorder has to do with body image concerns, especially those that take place early on in life.[8] If you or someone in your life expressed body image woes as a young child, you are more likely to fall into eating disorder patterns of behavior as you age. This may sound alarming, but it is also not an end all be all; not everyone who dislikes their body ends up with an eating disorder, even if the poor body image began as a small child. It simply makes one more likely to develop an eating disorder—it does not doom them to developing one. A way to combat this particular risk factor is to catch the behaviors early and to fight them with positive affirmations or therapy, both of which we will detail more in Chapter Four when we discuss treatment options.

Still more psychological roots of eating disorders could lie in the hearts of peer pressure and bullying over body size and shape.[9] This may sound almost too obvious or cliched to be a real reason behind an eating disorder, but the truth is that many younger eating disorder sufferers feel a great deal of pressure to conform to societal standards and norms set by their peers. When they aren't able to measure up, their peers often make sure that they know it, and publicly—bullying over how one looks is becoming increasingly common, especially now that it's possible to do it online. All of this is to say that eating disorders, while they may not ever be the fault of someone else, may certainly be influenced by the way that an individual is treated by those around them.

As is always the case, there may be more psychological elements to eating disorders that have yet to be discovered, just as there are with genetic and biological factors. However, the psychological factors are a bit easier to track, perhaps, because people are able to express what they are feeling in a way that the body is less able to communicate. There may be hope for more solid evidence and proof for the psychological causes of eating disorders if enough funding is given to research them.

Next up on our list of eating disorder causes is sociocultural factors. There are a variety of examples of sociocultural factors that go into eating disorders, and we will be discussing several of them in detail below so that you can get a solid idea of what constitutes a sociocultural risk.

Sociocultural Factors

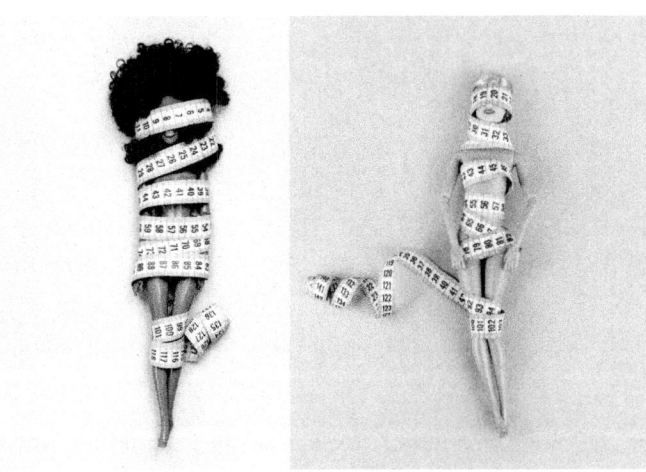

There is a wide assemblage of sociocultural factors that may contribute to an individual developing an eating disorder. It may first be helpful to define what we mean when we use the word *sociocultural*. Sociocultural is simply an anthropological term that refers to the intersection between the social and cultural worlds, and describes how they overlap. This can indicate anything from family and home life, to friends and coworkers, to media and other cultural factors, some of which we touched upon in our last section when we went over peer pressure and the negative effects it can have on young eating disorder sufferers. Now, it is time to address a particularly interesting eating disorder risk that is only *sometimes* a risk and is, in fact, somewhat a myth when it comes to being a risk at all: the family environment.

If you found that statement to be controversial, you likely would not be alone. However, an increasing amount of studies are showing that the home life of an individual contributes little to their risk of developing an eating disorder. Of course, there is a biological component that can automatically elevate the risk slightly, but researchers are finding that families are likely not to blame for eating disorders as often as one might suppose. When someone comes from an abusive household or a disordered eating environment, these things may factor in as trauma, but no longer are psychologists falling so frequently into the trap of "blaming the parents" for the eating disorder each time a child winds up developing one. We now know that there are a myriad of causes at play. While growing up in an abusive or dysfunctional household can absolutely increase stress levels of those at risk for developing eating disorders, we can now say with a fair amount of confidence that the family is, by and large, not to be held 100 percent accountable any longer.

Another scapegoat—although this one may be a bit more realistically at fault—is the cultural phenomenon of media. It's a near-worldwide issue that "thin" is the ideal body type, and not just generally fit, either; in some cases, models are truly skeletal, and it's what's being sold as desirable. The female mannequins in department stores are stick figures with bobble heads on top, their male counterparts sporting biceps and six-pack abs even though their jobs are to be modeling our clothing, not our ideal bodies. In movies, the actors and actresses all look the same: slim or fit, with very little room for body types that are in between. If anyone is heavy, they are typecast as comedic relief—God forbid they ever are given a serious role. We are bombarded with commercials featuring the rich and famous, telling susceptible people of all ages to purchase beauty products and clothes that won't make them look "fat" and any number of other things that are just as toxic. The point is this: although it can be flashy and fun, the media can be highly destructive to anyone, but especially someone who is likely to develop an eating disorder. Some argue that the media gets too rough a go of it when it comes to being blamed for eating disorders. Perhaps this is true. However, there is little doubt that eating disorders tend to take refuge in sources within the media.

Other sociocultural factors include being introduced to large amounts of stress, or even holding professions where weight loss is a common goal. An example of this sort of stress-inducing environment may be training as a dancer from a young age, just as Briana did, who we will meet at the close of this chapter. Another may be living in a household with parents who are perfectionists, though, as we know, this is not necessarily a trait that will rub off on a child or turn into an eating disorder in later life; it may simply raise the risk. The idea of a sociocultural factor here is that it is anything in the social or cultural life of an eating disorder sufferer that contributes to the manifestation of their disorder, which, as you are likely beginning to understand, can be any number of things. More researchers need to delve into the matter before all of the sociocultural factors behind an eating disorder can be uncovered, if such a thing is even possible. Each life and culture is so wildly diverse that it would take a vast amount of research, but that does not mean, of course, that it is not worthy of scientific attention or exploration.

We have examined, to the best of our ability, the genetic, biological, psychological, and sociocultural causes of eating disorders, though there is much left still to the imagination. Perhaps meeting Briana will help to shed some light on the subject for us. Within her story, Briana will allow us a view into what it is like to develop an eating disorder at a young age, just like Forest, though her tale is quite a bit different. Perhaps you will learn a little about what causes eating disorders through Briana's insight, and if you or someone you love has an eating disorder, you might see that recovery is a possibility through her eyes.

Briana's Story

Briana can't really recall what her life was like before the onset of anorexia nervosa. Although she acknowledges that her eating practices didn't become a full-blown eating disorder until she was around fourteen years old, it's difficult for her to remember a life without it; she just never realized that she had one. After everything you've read about anorexia, it might be tough to imagine not being aware that you have the disease, but

Briana's family culture revolved around a highly active, food-restrictive household. With a competitive figure skater for a mother and a cyclist for a father, the bar for healthy eating and extreme exercise was set high in Briana's home from day one. For a long time, Briana just thought that she was being athletic like her parents, not developing an eating disorder. It's an easy mistake to make.

Briana has memories of people commenting on her stature as early as seven years old. In her family, she was known as "Skinny Minny," and her small ankles were pointed out often. As a baby, she was so tiny that she was dressed in doll's clothes, something that her mother has brought up to her many times since. Being small was a part of the identity that was chosen for Briana, but her personality was anything but demure. She shares memories of a talkative, social childhood, but she was not always met with the listening ear she needed: she spent much of her time communicating with empty rooms or to a mother who tuned her out. She theorized that this could be where her feelings of being unheard first began.

Food rules first entered Briana's life when she was a child. She can remember her parents teaching her about "good" and "bad" foods, which might sound like ordinary parenting, but for Briana it was restrictive. She wasn't allowed to eat the same things as the other children she knew, though she did have something of a sweet tooth and, at this time in her life, was happy to indulge it when she could. Food rules played a major role in her life due to the nature of her own parents' eating and exercise regimens, and even though she did not consciously file away what her parents taught her as a way to control the size of her body, later on, she learned.

The eating disorder began to rear its ugly head when Briana was only in middle school. She hit puberty, and while everyone else was getting into boys, makeup, and fashion, Briana learned that the food rules in her family were reality, that she needed to diet in order to be worthy, and any number of other dangerous ideals that sent her spiraling down the eating disorder rabbit hole. While there is always a chance that she might have picked it up anyway, she expresses that she learned the concept of body hatred from her own mother, and it haunted her through middle school and beyond. She began to scrutinize her body and compare it to her peers, every last body part to which she had once been so oblivious in the past.

Briana danced. The world of dance can be extremely competitive, and many young men and women within it are primed for eating disorders at a young age. Unfortunately, Briana was no exception. She showed great promise in ballet, which she started in the summer before the eighth grade, and managed to get on pointe within six months. Although her fellow dancers may have been envious of her, Briana recalls that they also did not get their bodies publicly criticized in the same way that she did: the ballet master of the company team constantly hollered at her to "suck in her stomach," or told her that her that she could "never be a professional dancer because [her] quads and thighs were too big." Briana learned as she danced that the thinner girls got more solos, which clothes made her feel "fat" and which ones didn't, and how she could get by with eating less and less. These behaviors carried her through to high school, where things got nothing but worse.

Even though Briana found herself at a brand new school, she still felt like something of an outcast. She found more excuses to diet, overexercise, and restrict. An entirely new set of dance instructors were ready to critique her every facet, and she joined the dance team at her high school, thus scoring an in with the popular girls. Briana was still not interested in boys, but she was dating and simply doing what all of the other popular girls were. She didn't begin questioning her sexuality until her sophomore year, when she just couldn't understand why everyone seemed to be so crazy about relationships and she just . . . wasn't. She also began going to parties for the first time, as many people in high school do, but we also know that many individuals with eating disorders develop substance abuse issues alongside their conditions. Briana's substance abuse struggles didn't come until later. Instead, she struggled with a different behavior: self-harm.

Self-harm is not unique to individuals with eating disorders, and many people with other mental illnesses grapple with the behavior as well. For Briana, however, self-harm was a cycle that was directly related to anorexia. As she grew increasingly depressed and frail, she came to hate her body more and more. Not because she saw herself as too thin—she perceived herself as too fat (a perfect example of the body dysmorphia we covered earlier). She describes herself as losing her self-worth along with her "light" during this period in her life as she fell into a spiral of tracking her food intake in a journal, hating herself for it never being a small enough amount, and then self-harming as a form of punishment. Briana's world became one of darkness, self-inflicted pain, and hunger.

Finally, Briana couldn't take it anymore and reached out to an adult she trusted, knowing that what she was doing was a problem and that she needed help. She was put in therapy, but it was a miserable experience for her, and it did little to help her eating disorder. In fact, if anything, asking for help only served to make Briana sneakier in her behaviors. Now that her family and doctor knew that she had an eating disorder, she had to get more creative to stay thin. Her mental health continued to deteriorate as high school pressed on and junior and senior year rolled around. Her depression growing exponentially, and her weight continuing to plummet. Finally, she was admitted to San Francisco State University, and while you might suppose that going off to school might have offered a new start for Briana, it only offered an opportunity for her to engage in substance abuse behaviors. She wound up feeling unhappy at SFSU, so she transferred to the University of California, Davis for animal biology.

At UCD, Briana *did* get something of a new beginning. She felt confident, and her eating disorder behaviors were limited to orthorexia rather than severe anorexia, as they had been in the past. She spent hours dancing and working out at the aerial gym, which she had gotten into and developed a passion for during the lows of her junior year in high school, and found herself in the best shape of her life. However, all of this began to fall apart when her sexuality finally began to demand to be recognized. After years of being forced to reside under the surface of her consciousness, Briana began to come to terms with the fact that she was (and is) a lesbian. It was a painful realization for her, and she turned to her eating disorder again to cope. However, when she finally came out to her mother and dated her first girlfriend, she felt more aligned with who she was than she ever had before. Even when the couple ended up not being meant to be, things were okay . . . for a while.

And then came Lily. Briana reunited with a high school "one who got away" and quickly fell in love. The duo got engaged, and though Briana stayed committed, she found out that Lily had cheated, and the couple broke it off. Needless to say, this had a negative impact on Briana's mental health. She began to drink alone every night despite living at home with her parents, resumed self-harming, and reached an even lower weight than she ever had in high school. Her mother essentially forced her to go back to therapy, though Briana was extremely reluctant due to her previous negative experiences from high school. Regardless, she was fortunate enough to find a therapist she was able to bond with, and by the end of the year, she was back to a healthy weight once again.

After Lily, Briana dated a bit, but ultimately felt worthless and alone. As 2020 began and everyone was required to quarantine, she jumped at the opportunity to do some at-home workouts like many others who began to grow stir-crazy from being locked up. For Briana, however, her motivation went beyond losing a few pounds and improving her health: her anorexia wanted her to disappear. Drugs, self-harm, and restriction reentered the picture, and her eating disorder began to overtake her. In her own words:

The restriction got tighter and tighter, more foods became off-limits, my self-harm became more incessant and necessary, my drug use became a regular habit to avoid eating and getting annoyed with my life and friends, the body checking and dysmorphia went off the charts, and the satisfaction of losing weight right in front of my coworkers and therapist was rejuvenating. As my weight continued to drop, I found myself less and less able to eat in front of other people. I became hypervigilant of the habits of everyone around me. I became dependent on self-harm to control my emotions. I became increasingly irritable with those around me. I became unable to think about anything besides food and my body. I became unable to control my need to exercise. I became unable to sleep. I became less able to perform my job functions. I became less myself.

At long last, Briana realized that she needed help and needed to attempt recovery—for good this time. She came clean about her behaviors and sought support from her family, friends, and coworkers . . . at least initially. The trouble with anorexia is that it is extremely conniving, and even if the afflicted individual wants to recover, oftentimes the disease does not want to go. Even though her intent was to get better, her behaviors remained stronger than ever, and she continued to restrict, overexercise, and use drugs and alcohol to help shrink herself. It all finally ended when she had a spontaneous arrhythmia and a few other medical symptoms one day at work, and she was asked to go to urgent care to see a doctor.

Ultimately, the path Briana chose was to go to a residential treatment facility to help overcome her eating disorder. She remained there for some time, but her insurance eventually decided for her that it was time for her to go, and she was forced to step down to a Partial Hospitalization Program (PHP) away from the friends and staff who she had bonded with. The abrupt step down to PHP was difficult for Briana, and she initially didn't use her support system or eat outside of the program (we will cover how programs like Briana's operate in Chapter Five). She found herself self-harming and drinking again within a month of being cut from the residential facility, and was put "on contract," which is a term used in eating disorder treatment to describe a process in which high-risk patients are closely monitored by staff. She stayed in PHP for several months before transitioning to the next step down, an Intensive Outpatient Program, or IOP. While there, things got better. She still found herself struggling, but not as badly as before.

Today, Briana is back at work almost full-time, and though her eating disorder is not yet completely at bay, she is doing her best. Her depression and self-harm urges are still things that she battles with, but she continues to talk to her outpatient team (her therapist, dietitian, and psychiatrist) often. When asked how she sees her future, Briana says, "I know what this is, and I don't want it." She goes on to explain that she has lived almost her entire life with eating disorder behaviors, and that it's time to try something different.

No one is born with an eating disorder, but Briana has had to live a sizable portion of her life with anorexia nervosa. Raised in a household with food rules and body comparisons running the gamut, Briana may have been predisposed to developing her own obsessive nature with exercise and food, but it's difficult to say whether or not she would have been destined to have an eating disorder if she had been born into a different family with a more body-positive outlook. Whatever the case, Briana identifies her disorder in the form of restricting and overexercising behaviors that dog her to this day if she is not watchful, and, clearly, the process of removing these behaviors was a rocky one. Sometimes her eating disorder still creeps up on her, and she has phases when falling back into its arms sounds desirable even though she knows better. The most problematic issue of Briana's recent life was perhaps the fact that she was dumped from her treatment center prematurely due to her insurance deciding she was finished, as this separated her from a therapist she had truly connected with and friends that she remains in touch with to this day. This sent her into the spiral that resulted in the relapse that occurred while she was still in PHP, ending, of course, in her being put on contract. We will discuss how common it is for insurance to sever ties such as these in Chapter Five, but, fortunately for Briana, she is currently on the road to recovery.

Briana deserves to be more than a statistic, and if all goes well, she will be. If you are reading this and find that you identify with parts of her story, know that *you* deserve to be more than a statistic, too. We have mentioned multiple times in this chapter that if you or someone you know is suffering from an eating disorder, you should not wait to reach out for help. If you don't have someone in your life to turn to, try contacting the National Eating Disorder Association helpline, which is available through call or text at (800) 931-2237. Don't suffer in silence. Consider reaching out today.

FOUR

Who Gets Eating Disorders?

IF YOU'VE EVER HAD AN EATING disorder or disordered eating, one of the primary things you may know about the experience is that it can feel very isolating. Someone who has an eating disorder may feel like they are the only person in the world who is suffering from their behaviors, and they may think that there is something wrong with them that can't be fixed. However, the reality is that neither of these thoughts are true, no matter how powerful they are in the moment: eating disorders are more common than most people might realize, as we have learned, and they are very treatable with the right intervention (which is something we will be discussing in-depth in Chapter Five). But if that's right, then why is it that eating disorders can make those that struggle with them feel so alone? We know why people get eating disorders, or at least the theories. But who gets eating disorders, and is there anything we can do to prevent them?

The unfortunate truth is that eating disorders make sufferers lonely because they make them perform behaviors that drive them away from friends, family, and loved ones. Their social circles become smaller, and even though there are plenty of other people with eating disorders just like them all over the globe, it can become easy to feel like the only one. Alternatively, sometimes younger eating disorder sufferers connect with others with eating disorders on the internet, and this can be very dangerous . . . but we will circle back to this in its own section later in this chapter. For now, we will be examining who gets eating disorders.

Eating Disorders: Who Gets Them?

A regrettable state in which the current world finds itself is that anyone can develop an eating disorder. That isn't to say that no man, woman, child, or anyone in between is safe, of course, but the reality is that anyone can find themselves with an eating disorder if the circumstances line up just right (or wrong). However, according to the National Alliance of Mental Health, or NAMI, there are a variety of factors that can increase one's risk for developing an eating disorder. Many of them were not discussed as part of our previous chapter, so let us compendiously list them out and discuss them here instead:

- Age: One is more likely to develop an eating disorder in their teen years or early twenties, though it is possible to develop an eating disorder at any age. Remember: eating disorders do not discriminate.
- Gender: Girls and women are more likely than men to be *diagnosed* with an eating disorder, but that doesn't necessarily mean that they are more likely to have one; it may simply indicate a disparity in men and boys seeking treatment. Thus, it is

difficult to know for sure if women are much more likely than men to have eating disorders.
- Dieting: As we know, sometimes dieting can be taken to an extreme and can metamorphose into an eating disorder instead of a simple ploy to lose a few pounds here and there.
- Change: When changes occur in one's life, it can lead to stress, which can trigger eating disorder behaviors in individuals who are susceptible to them. These changes are usually major ones, such as moving away, or going through a divorce.[1]
- Professions and pastimes: It is not uncommon for eating disorders to appear among highly competitive jobs and activities, such as in ballet or sports.[2] As we saw in Briana's story, professional dancers can be extremely critical of other dancers' bodies, which can lead to low self-esteem and dieting behaviors in order to measure up to a preordained ideal. This is the case in many other vocations as well.

Although these factors may increase one's risk of developing an eating disorder, it is important to remember that eating disorders affect people of all races, shapes, sizes, genders, sexual orientations, and ages. The image that the media generally teaches the general population to think about when it comes to eating disorders is a frail caucasian teenage girl, and this is something of a myopic view when it comes to those who struggle with these conditions. As we explained in great detail over the course of Chapters One and Two, there is no one body type that makes an eating disorder an eating disorder, and supposing that only teenage girls can get them completely ignores entire demographics. We will be discussing several of these demographics next, including race, gender, sexual orientation and gender identity, and age. We have mentioned a handful of these same words above in the bulleted list, but we will be diving into them in much greater detail below, as there is more to say.

Eating Disorder Demographics

There are numerous facets that can lead an individual of any demographic to develop an eating disorder—this much we know. But who, specifically, is the most prone to getting eating disorders, and why? In this section, we will go over exactly who gets eating disorders besides the more open-ended "everyone" we have provided thus far.

Race:

When those with eating disorders are portrayed in movies or television shows, who are they usually played by? Very slight white actresses. This is not a universal truth, but it is very nearly one, so much so that even those who are non-white and struggle with eating disorders may not realize that they can have an eating disorder at all. In an interview with NPR, actor Karla Mosley of the daytime soap opera *The Bold and the Beautiful*, confessed that she didn't know that eating disorders weren't "rich white female adolescent disorder[s]," despite the fact that she had one herself.[3] Mosley is black and a full-grown woman, and doesn't fit the stereotypes that the media throws out for having an eating disorder. Many people don't, and find themselves adrift in a sea of eating disorder behaviors for a long time before they realize that it is possible for people like them to get eating disorders, too.

Black actors are not the only ones at risk for developing eating disorders that slip underneath the radar. In fact, the rates of eating disorders in minorities in general are quite similar to that of white women.[4] However, chances are that if you visit a treatment center, you will see many more white faces than you will see faces of color. It's a depressing truth that many minorities do not receive the help they need for their eating disorders, and this can be for a variety of reasons. Sometimes it can be almost cultural to have eating disorder behaviors, like it is among young women in Japan, where having an eating disorder is among one of the most common mental illnesses.[5] When being slim, petite, and demure is not only desirable, but is encouraged across an entire culture, it can be very difficult to embrace a body type that is larger than the "ideal" that may be presented by the media or even close friends and family members.

Japanese women aren't the only ones to develop eating disorders at the same rate as white women. In fact, it may be the case that people of color are *more* likely to develop eating disorders than their white counterparts due to environmental stressors like racism, poverty, and abuse.[6] An issue among eating disorder sufferers who are people of color is the problem of receiving care for their conditions once they realize that there is something to be done for the way they are feeling and behaving. Clinicians are less likely to listen to people of color than they are to white people, particularly black women; even in medical conditions that have nothing to do with eating disorders, black women are frequently ignored to the detriment of their health, and this occurs in the realm of eating disorders, too.

In summation, eating disorders occur just as frequently—if not more so—in people of color as they do in white people, and they should not be ignored. If you are a person of color and you have an eating disorder, try not to let the above paragraph deter you from seeking medical attention. Be persistent, and if one doctor doesn't listen, don't give up! Reach out to another clinician who specializes in eating disorders, preferably one who is a person of color themselves if you feel unsafe, as they may be less likely to discriminate.

Gender:

Just as eating disorders are primarily thought of as a white person's disease, they are certainly thought of as a woman's illness. No one thinks of a man when they imagine a person with an eating disorder, even though they are becoming increasingly prevalent among men. This is troubling for several reasons, not least of which is because when we stereotype—even accidentally or subconsciously—we cut out an entire portion of the population who might be struggling with an eating disorder, thus invalidating their pain. However, it is important to understand exactly where we got the idea that eating disorders are a woman's disease in the first place.

A brain study in 2016 attempted to shed some light on just that. This study, which was published in the scientific journal *Cerebral Cortex*, suggests that there may be biological reasons why women are seemingly predisposed to believe that they are inferior when it comes to body image. The long-standing hypothesis was that women were simply under more societal pressure than men to be beautiful, thin, and otherwise perfect in their appearances, but there may be more going on that leads to the fact that more women tend to show up with eating disorders than men. The study revealed that there may be neural pathways involved in making those with eating disorders like anorexia nervosa have a distorted sense of body image.[7] As it turns out, women may genuinely be predisposed to see themselves differently than men, based solely on the wiring within their brains. This is a possible explanation as to why eating disorders seem to be so much more common among women than men.

That being said, the reality that men face when it comes to eating disorders cannot be overlooked. Even though women might be more likely to develop eating disorders based on potential biological factors, men do face social pressures to conform to beauty standards, just like women. One could argue that men are not put under quite the same pressures or extremes when it comes to beauty standards as women; after all, no one is advertising male makeup products or expecting men to perform in beauty pageants. However, the truth remains that there are still societal standards that men feel burdened by, just as women do, and an eating disorder can be the end result of trying to fit into a role that someone isn't well-suited for.

Between 10 and 15 percent of anorexia and bulimia sufferers are male, and that's just out of those who are diagnosed.[8] Men frequently don't seek treatment for their eating disorders because it is seen as a feminine problem or, similar to the racial issue covered in the last section, they may not even realize that men are capable of having eating disorders because it is so widely advertised as a woman's disorder. They aren't, and if you are a man and are suffering from an eating disorder, you certainly aren't alone.

Sexual Orientation and Gender Identity:

Not dissimilar to the way that racism and poverty play into minorities' development of eating disorders, the stressors put on the LGBTQ+ community may increase their odds of getting eating disorders, too. According to the National Eating Disorder Association, twelve-year-old LGBTQ+ individuals may be at a higher risk for developing eating disorders than their heterosexual and cisgender peers.[9] This statistic may seem alarming, but considering the amount of trauma that the typical gay, lesbian, bisexual, or transgender person might have encountered to get to where they are today, and it isn't surprising to suppose that eating disorders might start early and that they might be more prominent.

Eating behaviors such as restricting and binge eating tend to be more common among the LGBTQ+ community when it comes to eating disorders, and there are a few reasons why this could be the case. Some researchers suppose that it could be because of the usual stressors that minorities have to contend with, which causes them to make poor decisions around food. Others argue that it is more complex than that, and has to do with the more specific issues that those in the LGBTQ+ community face, such as homelessness, gender dysphoria, coming out, discrimination, and more issues that can lead to unhealthy coping with an eating disorder. Whatever the case, the end result is that eating disorders tend to crop up more in the LGBTQ+ community than in the general population, though more research is needed to know for certain why this is.

Age:

It is no secret that eating disorders commonly show up in teenagers and other young people. But why is this the case? Is this actually true, or is this another stereotype that needs to be dispelled? Actually, this particular stereotype holds a seed of truth, though it is important to realize that not everyone who has an eating disorder is a teenager or anywhere near their youth. Some research suggests that the reason behind so many eating disorder sufferers being in their youth may be because puberty is a tumultuous time physically, mentally, and emotionally for many people, and susceptible individuals may turn to eating disorder behaviors to cope. The brain is also in a state of change during this period in human development, and it can cause wild fluctuations in hormone levels, mood, and perception that can seem insurmountable when one's only goals in life are to fit in and figure out who they are. If someone is predisposed to developing an eating disorder, this period in their life would be a prime time to do so.

But what about individuals who get eating disorders at an older age? Sometimes, middle-aged adults will try fad diets or will go to extremes to try to control their bodies and weights to avoid the natural changes that come with aging. Other times, eating disorder sufferers never get help in their youth, and their eating disorders continue throughout adulthood, making it less and less likely that someone might seek treatment as time wears on and a person gets more accustomed to their way of life. It's extremely important to recognize that not all people with eating disorders are in their teen years or younger, and that some may even be nearing retirement age, perhaps have even struggled with an eating disorder for years. While it's true that most eating disorders set in during a person's youth, this isn't the case for everyone, and they do not just vanish on their own as a person ages. A person cannot "grow out" of an eating disorder. These facts are not offered to frighten or discourage, but purely to inform. An eating disorder is an eating disorder, no matter the age of the afflicted individual.

Pro-Ana and Pro-Mia Websites

Depending on who you are and how experienced you are in the world of eating disorders, you may already be familiar with the concept of pro-ana and pro-mia websites. They are worth discussing in this chapter because not only do they contribute to people with eating disorders keeping them, but they may also play a role in susceptible individuals developing them in the first place, particularly teenage girls (and the occasional boy).

The terms *pro-ana* and *pro-mia* stand for *pro-anorexia* and *pro-bulimia*. It might surprise you to learn that such terms exist, but there truly are people out there who are so lost in their disorders that they believe that they are the "right" and "correct" ways of life, and that their behaviors are even worth passing on to others. For many people, diseases like anorexia and bulimia are lonely and isolating, but for those who engage in the highly toxic pro-ana and pro-mia circles, they have an entire community rallying around them that encourages them to keep their disorder as sickly as possible. These communities have message boards preaching special diets that promise the quickest results for losing the most weight, and special "ana coaches" who abuse and confuse followers into believing lies that can be lethal.

If you have an eating disorder, these communities can sound enticing and inviting, especially because it can seem like you finally have a group of people who understand what you are going through. However, you are far better off seeking help to get out of your disorder, not falling deeper into it. Alternately, if you discover that someone in your life has been visiting pro-ana or pro-mia websites, treat the issue with gentle concern and don't frighten them or shame them. Try to lend a listening ear and be a safe person to talk to, as chances are, that's what they're looking for more than anything by spending time in those chat rooms.

Are Eating Disorders Preventable?

We all want the answer to this question to be a resounding yes, but the fact of the matter is that it's not that simple. When it comes to whether or not eating disorders can be prevented, the short answer is yes *and* no. The long answer is a bit more complex. As we've learned (back in Chapter Three, to be exact) there are a variety of factors that go into developing an eating disorder, many of which we have yet to discover. Unfortunately, some of these would be difficult to prevent with our current understanding of medical science. One day, if we are able to isolate the specific genes and biological issues that switch on eating disorders, we might have a better chance of figuring out how to turn off those genes, if it is deemed ethically appropriate to do so. However, that isn't to say that there is no hope for eating disorder sufferers today. We can't forget about the environmental causes of eating disorders, which all affect people differently. If we catch eating disorder symptoms early on in their manifestation, we can treat them much sooner, thus allowing the afflicted individual to lead a long, healthy life.

This might not be quite the same as preventing an eating disorder, but perhaps the focus should be more on healing what we can when we can, rather than stopping eating disorders altogether, especially since the medical technology isn't there yet. This is not meant to be a bleak view, but a recovery-oriented view; eating disorders may not be possible to stop at the source today, but we can help sufferers get better as soon as they begin to show symptoms. For now, this is good enough.

We have discussed in detail who gets eating disorders, as well as provided some demographic information to help better illustrate what we mean when we say that eating disorders do not discriminate. We even examined the dark world of pro-ana and pro-mia websites, and explored the concept of whether or not eating disorders can be prevented. Now, it's time to meet Stacey, another young woman who volunteered to share her story with you. As a note, there may be some content in Stacey's story that is disturbing to readers with a history of sexual abuse.

Stacey's Story

Although Stacey describes her childhood as pleasant, she had a rough start to entering the world. She was her mother's first child, which resulted in a difficult labor, almost costing her mother's life. One of her friends from eating disorder treatment, upon hearing the story of Stacey's birth, jokingly referred to Stacey's entrance to the world as "rude." Stacey feels as though she must not have ever wanted to come into the land of the living in the first place. This may sound bleak and almost a tad pessimistic, but Stacey seems to feel frustrated about her birth.

Stacey's mother worked when she was young, so she was enrolled in a daycare called Head Start. She doesn't remember much about the program other than being told to be quiet and take a nap, but kindergarten is when she recalls being body shamed for the first time. Her first experience of being bullied also occurred in kindergarten, and would continue for many, many years afterwards. She had the same bully from this period of her life all the way through ninth grade, and she remembers that there would be many comments made from this particular tormentor about her stomach. She would also be accused of being a liar or of cheating, and no one seemed to listen to her no matter how much she tried to defend herself. Even as early on as this, she began to feel as though she didn't fit in with the rest of her peers. She learned for the first time that if she was quiet, then no one would pay attention to her, and she could escape her bullying to an extent.

During kindergarten, Stacey started therapy for the first time. She describes having to go because of poor behavior and frequent crying, though therapy was a miserable experience for her and didn't exactly comfort her. She would cry when she saw her therapist, and attempt to kick him. But time passed, and Stacey found herself in the third grade, where bullying had worsened and bodies were starting to grow and change. She was on the chubbier side in comparison to some of her other classmates, and there was an incident with a sweater that sticks with her to this day. Her bully from kindergarten took one of her sweaters and read the size—an extra large—out loud to the class, which was met with raucous laughter. Stacey and her mother attempted to get help from the guidance counselor after this, but nothing came of it.

In fifth grade, the bullying only grew worse, and Stacey began to fall into an early depression. As her body continued to change and she got her period for the first time like many of the other girls in her class, it marked the perfect opportunity to compare and despair. The girls at her school began to measure their bodies against each other, and it created a tempest of negative body image and self-hatred within Stacey. She became so miserable at school that she even attempted to run away from home and thought of never returning to school again, though this didn't pan out. And then the winter talent show rolled around. Stacey's class had to perform a dance, and her primary bully's mother was in charge. Stacey was called out in front of her class and told that she had to move to the back where she couldn't be seen because her frown was "saddening the performance." To this day, Stacey wonders why no one helped her if she was so visibly sad, and when she was walking home from school that afternoon, she contemplated suicide for the first time in her life. She stood on the edge of a bridge and sincerely thought about jumping, but in the end, all of the *what ifs* got to her, and she stepped away, choosing to go back home instead. No one noticed how utterly despondent she was, and she had never felt so completely unseen. The first of her eating disorder behaviors started that very same day: she began to purge.

When it came time for sixth grade, Stacey was thrilled. She was under the impression that she would be leaving behind her bullies when she went off to her new middle school, but that dream was swiftly shattered when many of them ended up in the same place as she did. She started exercising the summer before seventh grade started so that she could be fit for the new school year, though when it started, the bullying continued regardless. She began to self-harm for the first time, which, as we have seen, is fairly common among eating disorder sufferers, though Stacey's eating disorder had yet to become full-blown at this time in her life. She did manage to maintain one friendship, however, though her friend was also self-harming, and the two of them took refuge in this together.

The eating disorder reared its ugly head and became a true disorder for the first time as Stacey entered the eighth grade. She began to diet and exercise excessively with the intent to change her body, and her relationships with her family grew strained. She sorted foods into categories based on whether or not they were "good" or "bad," and began to lose weight. The more she self-harmed, the tighter her restriction became. School continued to be miserable due to bullying, but her new eating disorder behaviors began to make her feel oddly powerful . . . that is, until a routine trip to the doctor's office brought it all to a screeching halt. When the doctor noticed her weight, low blood pressure, and self-harm scars, they sent her straight to a hospital for two weeks to recover. Two weeks is not a very long time, especially to recover from an eating disorder, and Stacey didn't get better mentally. When she returned to school, she was assigned to a guidance counselor, who told her parents about her self-harm. They were extremely disappointed in her, but ultimately, she couldn't bring herself to stop.

Over the summer, Stacey's mental health continued to falter. She spent time in the psychiatric ward for her self-harm, depression, and anxiety, and even went to live with her aunt and cousins for a time to get away from her nuclear family. Ultimately, however, she was forced to go home and start the ninth grade, and when she did, everyone looked at her like she was a different person. She got lots of comments on her weight loss, though not many people knew what she had been through to make it happen. She ended up moving to a new city and leaving her school behind for a different one, and felt relieved to have a second chance at life. For a while, Stacey could honestly say that she was pretty happy.

And then things changed. When she came to a school counselor to talk about her stepfather sexually abusing her, her world turned upside down. She describes the events that transpired afterward the following way:

After talking to a therapist we fit in all the puzzle pieces, kind of. She told me I had most likely blocked out those memories from my mind to protect myself. Now I know that I would self-harm and engage in ED behaviors because of what my stepdad was doing to me.

The stress and trauma of going through such a scarring life event unearthed Stacey's eating disorder behaviors again, and she began to engage in self-harm once more to cope. She simply wasn't able to bear the burden of her mental and emotional wounds any other way. Prom and high school graduation came and went, but Stacey spent them exercising and skipped them both, feeling unworthy of attending. The restricting and exercising got so out of control that she even began to shame her family for consuming certain foods that were in her "bad" categories." It wasn't long after that when she was sent off to treatment one final time.

She went to an inpatient facility, which is the highest level of care available to eating disorder sufferers. It took her four times to get it right, and she was eventually *conserved*, a process we will go over in the following chapter. During her most recent stay in inpatient in 2020, she slowly worked her way down through the remaining levels (residential, partial hospitalization, intensive outpatient, and outpatient, all of which we will discuss in Chapter Five) and she finally completed her program.

Today, Stacey is not quite where she wants to be in terms of her eating disorder, but she is doing her best. She is actively working to educate herself about trauma, mindfulness, and recovery. She describes her current battle with her eating disorder as something that resembles a heartbeat monitor: there are days where she is doing quite well and other days when she is doing less so, but overall, she is okay. Some of the most valuable things she took with her from treatment were the friendships she made the last time she was there, as well as some of the tools that she continues to use to keep herself moving along a recovery-oriented path to this day. She sees a doctor, therapist, and psychiatrist regularly to help her manage her disorder, which is a common outpatient team. Finally, Stacey is learning to trust herself, and is becoming friends with the woman she has become. Despite her hardships, Stacey is grateful.

Stacey's story is harrowing, and although its ending may be imperfect, it is not an unhappy one. She is a survivor of violence, both self-inflicted and inflicted upon her by others, even from people who were supposed to care for her. This is not an unusual truth for eating disorder sufferers: Stacey's tale is uniquely her own, but as we learned back in Chapter Three, there is often a common denominator of trauma of some sort for those with eating disorders. If you are struggling with an eating disorder or know someone who is and has a trauma background, there are resources out there for you to utilize that can help. If seeing a therapist isn't feasible for you for one reason or another (perhaps you don't have insurance, or your schedule won't allow for it), there are numerous books out there for you to read that might be able to provide you with some tools to tend to your mental health. One such book is called *The Body Keeps the Score* by Bessel van der Kolk. Stacey is currently reading it, and it is helping her enormously. The book details how trauma is physically stored in the body and discusses methods by which it can be released. If you are looking for a place to start your healing journey and aren't sure where else to begin, this book could be a good jumping off point.

Always remember, whether it is as you're reading this book or as you are moving through life, that you don't need to suffer in silence or live through an eating disorder alone. As we move forward to discuss treatment options in the upcoming chapter, be sure to take advantage of each of the resources we provide, if necessary, as they apply to you. It's crucial not to leave yourself stranded on an island when it comes to coping with an eating disorder, and whether you are using the hotline we provided in Chapter One or any one of the treatment options we discuss in Chapter Five, make sure you are throwing yourself a life preserver and giving yourself an out.

FIVE

Treatment Options

WE HAVE MADE plenty of reference to this chapter throughout this book, and now it's finally time to discuss the treatment options available for those with eating disorders. Fortunately, there are many, and we will be going over each of them in great detail here as we explain how eating disorders are treated, what those treatment options look like, and how best you can utilize them if you need to. We will begin with a general overview of what the treatment options for an eating disorder are, and then we will dive into each of them and describe them in more depth.

Treatment Options: An Overview

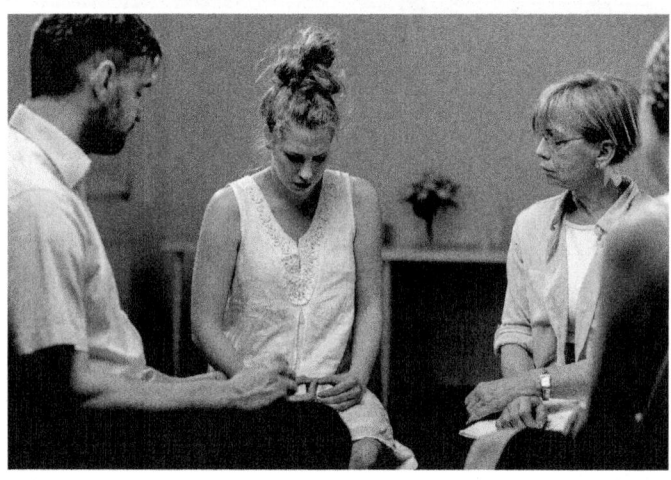

When you or someone you love is in the midst of an eating disorder, the situation can feel utterly hopeless. The good news, however, is that eating disorders are quite treatable when they are tackled with the proper tools and therapies. These tools and therapies include a solid amalgamation of psychological therapy, medical monitoring, nutrition education, and perhaps even medication, depending on a case-by-case basis.[1] It is important to remember that it is not always necessary to seek hospitalization for your or your loved one's eating disorder, though that is, of course, an option that we will be discussing later on. While hospitalization may be necessary if the health effects of the eating disorder have gone too far or if the eating disorder has become otherwise too advanced, there are other options available for treatment, too.

Let's, for now, assume that you are not going to immediately seek out hospitalization for your eating disorder and are going to first try other avenues of care. If this were the case, you might look for a registered dietitian, a physician, a psychiatrist, and a psychotherapist to form an outpatient team to help you combat your eating disorder symptoms. If that sounds overwhelming, don't worry; we will be providing resources within this chapter to help you on your search for medical professionals, if you need to find them. The best way to get going on assembling a team to care for you and your eating disorder (or the eating disorder of your loved one) is to get a referral from a physician or mental health professional to a team who specialize in eating disorder treatment. This is extremely important: you don't want to simply hire a therapist who is a marriage and family counselor. They need to also have experience in dealing with eating disorders, as eating disorders are a highly specialized field that not every professional has the expertise for.

Once you have assembled your outpatient team, you will begin regularly seeing each doctor, therapist, or psychiatrist as you recover. These visits will not be for the short term, and you can expect to continue to see each of these professionals for the course of the next several months or even years as you carry on with your recovery journey. Therefore, you should do your best to make sure that you find care that you feel safe and comfortable around. None of this talk about how long it can take to recover is meant to discourage or belittle, of course; simply keep in mind that recovery is often a gradual process, and you ought to find professionals that you don't mind seeing repeatedly as time passes and you move forward along your path to recovery.

Now, let's assume that you skip this step and seek out hospitalization first instead of trying to go at it with an outpatient team. This is also a perfectly valid way to go about treating your eating disorder. Each eating disorder has different requirements for care, as each person who has one has different behaviors that vary in severity. Thus, some people with eating disorders go straight to inpatient hospitals, or some do partial hospitalization programs—both of which we will be covering a little later on in the chapter. There are additional levels to hospitalization that we covered in Chapter Four during Stacey's story, but we will tackle each of those later on as well. For now, let's sink our teeth into what the picture looks like if you choose to go to treatment and move forward from there.

When you've chosen to go to treatment, you will have to select a treatment facility. We will go into much more detail about what this looks like and how to handle the process later on in the chapter, but for now it will suffice to say that you may want to select one that is either in your area or takes your insurance, or both—whichever best suits your needs. If you are starting from inpatient, you will begin in a hospital setting. Then, when you are ready, you will graduate to a residential facility somewhere else, perhaps even in another state, depending on what the care in your area is like or what you can afford. Gradually, you will work your way down through the partial hospitalization and intensive outpatient programs, and, finally, you will return home where you will have an outpatient team waiting for you so that you can continue treatment from the comfort of your own home and test your treatment skills. All of this can take a few months to over a year to complete; it is quite individualized and depends on your schedule, insurance, and eating disorder prognosis. Some people are able to complete treatment in a matter of months, while others go back and forth for years. It all depends on you and what you are up against.

Now that we have given you a sense of what to expect in reading this section, it's time to initiate our first topic of real discussion: outpatient treatment and all that it entails. We will be going over everything from how to find doctors if you are starting from square one, to what kinds of therapies work best for eating disorders. We may even recommend a book or two along the way. So, let's dive into which outpatient treatment options may be right for you or your loved one if you're suffering from an eating disorder and you're ready to tackle it.

Choosing Outpatient Treatment

How your outpatient journey begins depends on a variety of factors, but an important one is whether or not you start out in therapy or already have a physician you are seeing. Perhaps these are for issues that are seemingly unrelated to your eating disorder (though, chances are, they are more closely intertwined than you might initially realize) but the fact that you are seeing professionals already is a positive step in the right direction that can set you up for an easier transition into eating disorder treatment. As we've already covered, you will need several people on your new medical and mental health team to help get you back on track, including:

- A registered dietitian: A registered dietitian is someone who can use their knowledge of food and science to help you plan out a healthier future for yourself when it comes to how you approach food. They may do this by working with you to create meal plans, helping you to challenge food rules, doing exercises called *food exposures* with you, during which you challenge your negative food beliefs, and more.
- A physician: A good physician can be tough to come by, especially one who treats eating disorders with the gentle understanding that they deserve. Therefore, if you have a physician that you feel close to, keep them in your life and use them to refer you to the rest of your outpatient team (we will go over the referral process momentarily). When it comes to eating disorder treatment, your physician will monitor your weight restoration progress (if this is part of your eating disorder) and will care for any maladies that they are qualified to look after (though sometimes you may be referred to a specialist).
- A psychiatrist: Just like your physician, it can be difficult to come by a psychiatrist who truly knows and understands the plights of those with eating disorders. However, it is far from impossible, and if you have tried and failed to find one so far, you shouldn't give up just yet. Psychiatrists are there to provide medications for mental illnesses, but a good one will also listen to your problems and will medicate accordingly and only when necessary. If you don't yet have a psychiatrist, try calling your insurance to see who they will cover and compare reviews of both the doctor and their staff online to narrow down your choices.
- A psychotherapist: A good therapist can feel like a best friend when it comes to battling your eating disorder. They may also

feel like your worst enemy at times, depending on what your therapeutic homework of each session is, if it is your therapist's style to assign any. It is your therapist's job to see through your eating disorder's games, tricks, and lies, even the ones that you might not realize are there. However, it is important to remember that therapy only works if you go home and do the work. Your therapist cannot help you if you are not willing to implement the tools they provide you with in each session.

- Your friends, family, and other support people: This is an essential component to any outpatient or inpatient team. Those you love and care about are arguably your most important allies throughout your entire recovery process, more so than even your medical and mental health professionals, because they are the ones who will remain by your side even after treatment is over and you are ready to resume your everyday life, eating disorder–free. If you don't currently have many people in your life who you feel supported by, that's okay; there is always time to build up a better circle of friends or to develop your relationship with your loved ones. It might even give you something to focus on in your recovery other than your eating disorder.

As you can plainly see, there are many things to take into consideration when choosing your outpatient team and getting to know the medical—and nonmedical—professionals in your life. But what about if you don't currently have any medical care to speak of, and you have to start from square one when it comes to assembling your outpatient team?

The first step you may want to take when assembling your outpatient team, if you are starting from scratch, is to determine how much time you have. How advanced is your eating disorder, and should you be considering inpatient rather than outpatient treatment? Something that is extremely important to remember at all stages of an eating disorder is that if you think you may have a problem, you probably do. There is no such thing as an eating disorder that isn't a big deal, or that shouldn't be taken seriously because you aren't sick enough yet. You are always sick enough to get the help you need. When we ask you to consider how much time you have left, it isn't meant to be a frightening measure or a scare tactic:

it's meant to be used as a method to ground yourself and determine whether inpatient or outpatient care is ultimately right for you.

If you have settled on outpatient treatment, it is time to find a doctor who specializes in eating disorder care. As we stated above, finding a doctor who can treat eating disorders can be tricky, but it is far from hopeless. Take advantage of resources like the NEDA helpline that we provided at the end of Briana's Story, at the end of Chapter Three. Not only can you call to receive information about eating disorders, but they may be able to guide you in next steps towards finding a physician who can help you with your medical care and referrals to the rest of your team.

When it comes to taking concrete steps to finding a physician, start at your local hospital or family general practitioner. It's possible that they may not be eating disorder experts, but they'll be able to give you a check-up and point you in the right direction when it comes to who you can see who *will* be able to help you heal from your disorder. You'll need to get referrals from your doctor to see these other members of your future outpatient team, which is a fairly straightforward process. You will simply want to make an appointment with your physician to discuss eating disorder treatment on an outpatient basis, and they can help you from there. Make sure you are open and honest about your behaviors; even though it can be extremely difficult to be transparent about what you are dealing with due to the secretive and shame-based nature of eating disorders, you are only prolonging your illness if you keep details to yourself. By putting everything in the open, you will be giving your doctor a more accurate picture of exactly what it is you are going through, and they can refer you to someone who can help you heal accordingly.

After you get your referrals, one of two things can happen. It may be up to you to contact the professionals you are being referred to, or your physician may do it for you. If the latter option is the case, then it will require you to be patient and hang in there to the best of your ability while you wait for the new members of your team to begin getting back to you. If it takes more than a week, don't be afraid to follow up with your doctor and make sure that they remembered to make the calls or enter the referrals into their system (if they are electronic). Sometimes, physicians get so busy that they need a reminder in order to complete the referral process, and there is no harm in making sure that they are getting the work done on their end. You want to get your team assembled as quickly as possible to avoid changing your mind or deteriorating in health, so remember: sometimes it pays to be a squeaky wheel, as those are the ones that get the most attention. And when you need help, there's no shame in asking for it.

Finally, you will hear back from each of your new medical and mental health professionals (or, if you made the calls yourself, the waiting game might be a little shorter depending on if you were able to get ahold of them on the first try). Now, it's time for an initial consultation. Some therapists, dietitians, and doctors prefer to do these in person, but others will do them over the phone or over video call—it all depends on the professional and their practice. Each consultation or initial visit will usually last around an hour, and will consist of paperwork (unless you are able to fill it out online prior to the appointment) and a great many questions from the professional. These questions will vary depending on who you are seeing, but no matter what, you should do your best to be as open and transparent as possible. If you feel a good connection to each of these individuals, they will be in your life for the duration of your recovery (and maybe longer), so it's best to let them in to the best of your ability.

Something that is fair to note is that you do not have to stick with any of the professionals that your physician refers you to if you do not like them. You can always seek out a different therapist, dietitian, psychiatrist, or even doctor if something about them just doesn't feel right. It's important that you feel safe and comfortable around your outpatient team, because recovery doesn't end when your behaviors stop happening; it's a long process that can carry on for years at a time, especially if you have comorbid disorders to address. Make sure that you feel right around your team before committing to anyone, and don't worry about hurting feelings if someone isn't right for you: they're there to help you, not the other way around. Choose a team that will benefit you for the long haul, and you and your recovery will be secure.

Choosing Inpatient Treatment

Inpatient treatment is, in some ways, a completely different animal than outpatient treatment. They have their similarities, of course; after all, you will have the same type of team, with some additional support depending on which level of care you choose. However, inpatient treatment is, as you might suppose, quite a bit more intensive than outpatient treatment in terms of hours and therapies offered during the day, and you will not have access to your same outpatient team (meaning, you will temporarily have to use a different therapist, dietitian, psychiatrist, and doctor provided by the facility at which you are attending). For some eating disorder sufferers, the thought of leaving behind their current therapist or dietitian (if they have one) is frightening, but inpatient treatment has its benefits if that's the level of care that you need. But how do you determine if you need inpatient care, and when do you know if it's the right choice for you?

Choosing any level of care is always a very personal, individualized decision. However, there are a few things to look for in yourself that might make the choice a little easier:

- Outpatient just isn't working: One of the first signs that trying inpatient might be the best way to go for you is that your other forms of treatment aren't proving effective. Perhaps you started out with outpatient and gave it your all, but you just aren't seeing the improvements that you or your team is hoping for. Or maybe you've been in outpatient for a while and just can't find the motivation to give yourself the push you need to take your treatment seriously, and you need more encouragement to help get you on track. Whatever the case is, you may find that the more regimented version of treatment that an inpatient treatment center can offer may be more helpful to you.

- Your physical symptoms are getting out of hand: If your health is going downhill and you aren't certain where else to turn, an inpatient treatment center might be exactly what you need. In this case, going straight to the hospital for a few weeks might be the initial step, and, once you are well enough, you may then step down to a less intense level of care called residential. As you will discover in the next section, your medical situation will still be monitored when you are in residential, but as you will no longer be in a hospital setting, the care will not be as comprehensive.
- Your comorbid disorder(s) are getting out of hand: If you have depression, anxiety, OCD, or any other disorder that is making living with an eating disorder even more difficult than it needs to be, going to an inpatient treatment facility may be the appropriate next step for you. This can be tricky, because sometimes your underlying or co-occurring conditions can be contributing to your eating disorder or making it worse, or other times they may simply be tacked on as additional hardships that you have to deal with that have little to do with the eating disorder itself. A good treatment center will know how to handle your comorbid disorders with care and understanding, and will be able to get to the root of what is bothering you and causing your eating disorder and other symptoms to manifest. This is not always something that you can find in outpatient care, because it can require observation to get to the bottom of everything that is going on with you, and your outpatient team may not be able to watch over you.

So, if you've chosen inpatient care you may be wondering what to do next. How do you find a treatment center? Do you need a referral to get into one, or can you simply pack up and go? And what levels of care are there? We touched on them briefly in Stacey's story, but we will go over them again shortly. Let's start at the beginning, just as we did with outpatient treatment, and we'll walk you through the process of inpatient treatment.

Once you've settled on inpatient, you need to determine which level of care you need. There are several levels of treatment that you can try. As a refresher, the levels of care you can choose from are *inpatient* (hospitalization), *residential, partial hospitalization programs* (*PHPs*), *intensive outpatient programs* (*IOPs*), and, of course, *outpatient*. Let's dive into each of them in a little more depth so you have a sense for what each of them looks like— that way, you can make a more educated decision about which level of care is most appropriate for you or your loved one:

- Inpatient (hospitalization): For the purpose of this book, we use the term *inpatient* to refer to both this type of hospitalization and the generalized category of treatment that is a step above the outpatient level. Inpatient treatment is the most intense form of treatment available to eating disorder sufferers, and can be used as either a first or last resort, depending on the path you choose for your recovery. If you opt for inpatient treatment, you will find yourself in a hospital, so the setting will be quite clinical. There will be medical care available to you around the clock, and you will be very closely observed. This may sound scary, especially because it can make it more difficult to act on eating disorder behaviors, but you are there to heal and recover, and your desire to do these things will, ideally, carry you through. The length of inpatient treatment can vary, and it depends on how well you are responding to treatment both physically and mentally. Sometimes people are there for a few weeks to stabilize, and other times they may be there for months at a time. It all depends on you. If your stay is longer, try not to get discouraged, as it doesn't mean you are failing at your recovery: everyone's recovery is different, and you are allowed to take your time. The most important thing is that you truly recover and that you don't try to rush things.

- Residential treatment: Residential is the next step down from inpatient treatment. At a residential treatment center, you may live in a converted home or residence—hence the name. This version of treatment is much more therapy-focused and less clinical than inpatient, as by this point you are likely mostly medically stable, though you may still be on activity restrictions and your life will be largely sedentary. In residential, you will participate in individual and group therapy, and relearn how to eat, exercise, and treat yourself. You may or may not share a room with someone, depending on the size and stipulations of your facility. This can be a remarkable opportunity to bond with someone who shares a struggle with you, whether that comes in the form of your eating disorder or something else entirely. You will be under supervision for most of the day, particularly before and after mealtimes, but it will be looser than if you were in inpatient.
- Partial Hospitalization Programs: When you are ready to graduate from residential treatment, chances are that the recommendation from your medical and mental health professionals will be to go to a PHP. It's possible that the same treatment center you are in will offer PHP and IOP programs as part of the same center, but there's also a chance that you may have to look elsewhere for treatment. When you are in PHP, you can expect to dedicate up to eight hours a day, five days a week to your treatment at a center or, if you enroll in a virtual program, online. To start out, your team may have you prepare at least two of your meals at the program with the supervision of staff, and, as you learn how to portion again, you may be asked to start bringing in food with you for the staff to approve. Like with residential treatment, you can expect to participate in group therapy, family therapy, individual therapy, and various therapeutic activities that are designed to help you get your eating disorder straightened out and your life back on track. Some people start off with PHP and never need inpatient or residential, so keep PHP in mind if you're not certain that you need the intensity of a higher level of care.

- Intensive Outpatient Programs: IOP is the last level of care available to eating disorder sufferers before they get down to outpatient treatment. In IOP, you will likely be in the same treatment facility as you were for PHP, except your hours and days of treatment per week are reduced. How much they are reduced depends largely on your program and how well you are doing in treatment, and it can change over time as you continue to improve. At this level of treatment, you will likely be responsible for all of your own meals, though this may vary depending on the treatment center you are in (some may want to provide lunch for you). Once you get close to graduating IOP, your team will help you set up an outpatient team if you do not already have one.

Now that you have a snapshot of each of your treatment options, you might have a better feel for which level of care you might like to pursue. Once you're set on your level of care, it's time to look at treatment centers. There are a few ways to go about doing this. You may want to simply sit down with your computer and look online for treatment centers that offer types of therapy that look appealing to you (we will cover some of the most common forms of these a little later on). You can also call your insurance to see what they will cover. However, perhaps the most common way to find a treatment center is to pick one out and let them do the work for you. There are countless treatment centers available, and you do not necessarily have to limit yourself to one in your area if the care or reviews for that center look substandard. Plenty of eating disorder sufferers will travel across the country if need be in order to receive the care they need; sometimes a change of scenery can be helpful in the healing process, and it can be good to get away from the familiar area where you act on your behaviors.

Make a list of all of the treatment centers that look like places you might like to go and research them. Look at reviews, but try not to take them to heart if they complain about things like the food or a particular activity being difficult. Remember that the reviews are being written by people who do not necessarily want to be at the center, so it's important to parse through them to find reviews that are well balanced and not necessarily griping about the difficulties of the treatment process. When you've found a handful of treatment centers or even just one treatment center that sounds like a good fit, start making calls. Sometimes, you can contact the center through an online form, and they will get back to you as soon as possible. No matter what, however, you will likely have to speak to someone on the phone. Try not to worry if this isn't your forte: chances are that whoever you will be speaking to will be extremely kind and understanding of your situation, and will want to help.

Next, the treatment center will arrange for a phone consultation with you to gather insurance information and some background about you and your eating disorder. They'll want to know everything you can tell them about your behaviors, about what brought you to seek help, and about your eating disorder as a whole so they can get an idea as to whether or not you need the level of care you are looking for. Sometimes, the treatment center may recommend a higher or lower level of care based on what you share, but it is always up to you to decide what you need. You are in the driver's seat of your recovery, especially because at the end of the day, a treatment center is also a business, and they need you just as much as you need them. They are unlikely to turn you away, so if you are worried that you are not "sick enough" to look at a higher level of care, do your best to remember that the worst thing that can happen is that you graduate quickly from your program and move down to a level of care that may better suit your needs.

After your consultation ends, you will have to be patient while your treatment center's staff rushes around behind the scenes to run your insurance and negotiate, if necessary, to get you into treatment as quickly as possible. In the meantime, they will want you to get some paperwork and medical documentation filled out to send in to them. You will need to make an appointment with a physician to get an EKG and some blood work done (such as a Complete Metabolic Panel, or CMP), and possibly other tests depending on what your insurance needs to see to prove you are in need of treatment. All of this will need to be turned in within a few weeks—or perhaps even days—of you being admitted to your new treatment center.

From the moment you make the first call or email to the day you are admitted, it can be a whirlwind of an experience. Some people wait virtually no time at all before they are admitted to a treatment center, and others are waitlisted for months at a time. It all depends on your insurance, your medical situation, any complications you might have from your eating disorder, and the availability of space at the treatment center. There are certain times of year that are worse for eating disorder treatment centers than others in terms of crowdedness, particularly around the holidays and other food-centric celebrations, so if you know that there are annual times that make your eating disorder harder, this may be something to be conscious of when seeking inpatient treatment.

A Day in the Life of Residential Treatment

Although we will be meeting Stella for the first time at the end of this chapter, Forest will be revisiting us to describe a day in his life at his last treatment center. Through this story, you will be able to get a taste for exactly what it is like to experience a higher level of care. Keep in mind that Forest's story is meant to be used as an educational tool and not as a benchmark for what every residential treatment center is like.

Every morning at five or five thirty, the nurse on duty comes into Forest's room to wake him up and take his vitals. This routine consists of him lying down in bed while she takes his blood pressure, then sitting up while she does the same. Sometimes, she wants his standing blood pressure, too, but not typically. After that, he has to get out of his pajamas and change into a gown so he can go downstairs to be weighed.

It may seem odd that a treatment center would want to put any focus whatsoever on patient weight, but weight restoration is a necessary step in the recovery process for many people. It is unlikely that your treatment center will tell you what you weigh (and they shouldn't, as this can lead to an unhealthy fixation on weight that is detrimental to the healing of your eating disorder) but they will weigh you once a day when they take the rest of your vitals in the morning, just like they did with Forest. The reason for this is twofold: they will want to make sure you are making physical progress if weight restoration is part of your journey, and insurance will want to see that your weight is either moving in an upward direction (if need be) or is remaining stable. Insurance is highly focused on the physical health aspect of eating disorders and much less so on the mental health facets, which has a negative impact on many eating disorder sufferers (eating disorders, as we have learned, originate in the mind, not in the body).

After the weighing process and the rest of the vitals are complete, Forest usually troops back upstairs to where his room is in the house to try to get a half hour more of sleep or take a shower, depending on which day of the week it is. Because Forest is the only male in his residential facility, he has a room to himself. There are other residents in the house with their own rooms, though who gets a single room and who gets roommates is decided on a first come, first serve basis. Forest's facility is set up so that each bedroom has its own bathroom, and it is a two-story complex with several other small buildings arranged around a small courtyard. The main house is where Forest and the rest of the patients eat, sleep, bathe, and spend their free time. This is also where Forest marches downstairs in the morning at around six thirty or six forty for the second time every morning to return to the nurse's station once again.

In residential, you do not have access to medication, sharp objects, or certain bath and beauty products, so you must check them out from the nurse's station. The nurses, who rotate shifts on a daily basis, will also dole out medications to you as needed. So, when he goes downstairs the second time to stay, Forest takes his medication and then goes to the living room to hang out with his friends, who are also filing downstairs. At this point in his treatment, he is making breakfast for himself, so he waits to be called into the kitchen for portioning.

At this treatment center, portioning is a privilege that each patient needs to work up to with the permission of their dietitian. Only two meals a day are portioned (lunch is always portioned for each patient, no matter how far along in treatment they are), which helps to keep things on schedule, as portioning can take a little while. It may seem strange that a treatment center would want to keep its patients away from food, but sometimes it can be overwhelming to measure out food in its proper amount with the expectation that you will have to consume it, or other times the eating disorder is just too strong and your dietitian knows that you may attempt to over or under portion your plate. It can take time before playing with food again is a good idea and isn't just stressful or scary, so this is why Forest had to earn the privilege of portioning and prove he was ready.

After portioning and breakfast, which lasts for approximately a half an hour at this particular treatment center, Forest and the rest of the patients (of which there are perhaps seven) head off to a different building to participate in their first hour of group therapy. In this group, someone is sharing the story of how their eating disorder came to be, which is an experience that you may or may not have to go through at your treatment center. Forest listens quietly and, before he knows it, group ends and it is time for the first break of the day, which occurs at ten o'clock. Snack is at ten thirty, which he is also expected to portion for himself at this point in his treatment.

Most eating disorder treatment centers will have you eat a total of six times a day. This may sound excessive, especially if you are used to not eating at all, but they are not full meals: you will be eating three meals and three small snacks. The purpose of this is to restart your metabolism and to reintroduce nutrition into your body, not to mention that it will help to normalize food for you again. You may feel as though you are overeating for a time, but rest assured that your team is monitoring your physical progress and are doing everything in their power to keep you healthy and safe. If your feelings of being overly full do not go away—or, conversely, eating again restarts your appetite and you begin to feel hungrier—talk to your team and they may adjust your portion sizes for you. However, be sure that it's really you making the request and not your eating disorder.

Once snack wraps up, it's time for more group therapy. This time, the focus is on cognitive behavioral therapy, or CBT. We will talk more about what CBT is in the next section, but it is a popular form of therapy in eating disorder treatment facilities. A therapist leads the group, and there may be a handout to follow along with to help patients remember the lesson. Forest takes notes.

After this group ends, it's time for lunch. As previously mentioned, there is no patient portioning for lunch, so it is served quickly and takes about a half hour to eat. There is always time built in after each meal in case patients are unable to finish within the allotted time frame for meal supplementation. This typically takes the form of either Ensure or Boost, and the staff will measure out how much is appropriate to drink based on how much of the meal was eaten by the patient. The supplement must be consumed in its entirety, or eventually consequences will have to be faced (these may include going to a higher level of care if it happens often enough). Forest manages to finish his lunch most of the time these days, and today is no exception.

When lunch is through, Forest meets with his individual therapist instead of joining his peers for another round of group therapy. They discuss some of the things from Forest's past, and it is a productive visit. Individual therapy is one of the key aspects to eating disorder treatment, and at this level of care, it occurs three days a week. One of these days may be dedicated to family therapy, if you choose that you would like it to be part of your care plan—not everyone wants or needs their family to be involved with the treatment of their eating disorder. Forest took advantage of both when he was in residential, but what you do with your treatment is up to you.

The rest of the day progresses much the same way: When therapy ends for Forest, it's time for a break before he is expected to portion his afternoon snack. He spends the break socializing and spending time in the courtyard, enjoying the afternoon sun. When snack ends, it's time for a final group for the day before dinner. Forest and the rest of the patients head back to the group room and settle in for Nutrition Group, where they learn about the science behind food from a registered dietitian. In your nutrition groups, you may simply have a discussion for an hour, or you might play a game of sorts that requires some light physical activity, depending on what everyone's exercise clearance level is like. Forest happens to dislike games, so he was relieved that this day was a day of note-taking and lecturing rather than playing anything competitive.

At last, the day begins to draw to a close. Forest portions his dinner, eats, and waits around in the living room for movie night to start. It's his favorite night of the week, because the last group of the day has been replaced with a much more amusing movie evening rather than something educational, which he is never quite in the mood for after dinner. He settles in for the movie, which the group pauses halfway through to portion and eat the evening snack (while watching the movie, if they so choose), and, once it's over and he is off observation for the night, he heads upstairs to bed.

Observation is the last thing we will cover in this section before moving on to our discussion of the therapeutic treatment options that are available for you in treatment centers. Often nicknamed "obs," observation is simply what it is called when each patient is observed for varying hours after every meal and snack. They may not be allowed to fully close the door when using the bathroom or to flush the toilet once they have finished, as they may be a risk for purging. However, as time goes on and the patient in question earns trust, they will be permitted to close the restroom door, flush the toilet, and go upstairs (if such a thing applies to the facility) at their leisure for bedtime because they have proven that they will not act on any eating disorder urges should they arise.

So, there you have it: a day in the life at residential. With luck, this will help to elucidate what it may look like for you to spend a day in residential, yourself. Just as we stated before, keep in mind that this account is only a single day out of many other days in Forest's treatment, and his experience cannot be used as a ruler by which to measure your own. Each recovery is unique and no treatment center is quite the same as its neighbor.

Therapeutic Treatment Options

You now have a feel for the two broader types of treatment that you can choose (inpatient or outpatient) and have read a detailed account of what it was like for Forest to live at his last treatment center. Therefore, you are ready to read about some of the types of treatment that are used at treatment centers, many of which you are likely to encounter on your own recovery journey (or your loved one's). Below are listed some of the most common forms of therapeutic approaches to treating eating disorders:

- Cognitive Behavioral Therapy: Cognitive behavioral therapy, also known as CBT, is a type of therapy that is designed to help you get to the root of unhelpful thought patterns. In CBT, you will work with a therapist in a structured way through a set therapeutic curriculum of sorts. You will learn about cognitive distortions, strengthen your interpersonal skills, and develop ways to put an end to problematic behavior before it starts. It's the foundation of most types of therapy you will find in treatment centers, and you can expect to grow quite used to it as you begin to settle in to therapy.
- Dialectical Behavioral Therapy: Dialectical behavioral therapy, or DBT, is a very popular form of therapy in the world of healing mental health disorders, and was originally designed for

treating borderline personality disorder. It's a form of therapy that was developed from CBT, and focuses on regulating emotions, mindfulness, and interpersonal relationship skills. The term "dialectical" comes from the notion that combining two opposing ideas—such as acceptance and change—and in therapy, this can lead to desirable healing results. DBT is not taught in every treatment center, but it tends to be highly effective when it is combined with the treatment of comorbid disorders.

- Acceptance and Commitment Therapy: Acceptance and commitment therapy, or ACT, is the third acronym that you can expect to grow familiar with during your time in treatment. Not every treatment center will teach ACT outright because many of its principles are covered by DBT, but it is certainly worth noting here because you may not want to be caught unawares by a new form of therapy you've never heard of during your first time in treatment! ACT is all about accepting your emotions as they come and committing to not feeling guilt or shame about the form they take. It leans heavily on mindfulness practices, and encourages patients to face problems head-on so they can respond to their stressors in the most appropriate manner possible. It isn't as widely used as either CBT or DBT, but it is still quite a helpful and useful therapy for many people on a daily basis.
- Exposure Therapy: Exposure therapy is a form of therapy that you will absolutely run into during your time in eating disorder treatment. Chances are that it will be a tough one for you to work through at the time (it's designed to be), but you'll be glad to have done it when you're on the road to recovery. The point of exposure therapy is, essentially, exactly what it sounds like: you will be exposed to many of your fear foods (and perhaps certain forms of exercise, depending on what you agree upon with your team) in a controlled setting with the support of a therapist or dietitian to help you get through the experience. Depending on the exposure, you may simply be portioning, touching, or interacting with the food. Other times, you will be eating it. It all

depends on you and what kind of a challenge your team is setting up for you on that particular day. You will never be asked to do more than you can handle, and if you feel like you are being exposed to too much, you can always speak up for yourself and ask for a different exposure. Just remember that you are going to have to be exposed to the food or exercise at some point in the future again if you want to truly recover, and that treatment is a good place to encounter it because you'll be surrounded by all the support you need.

- Group Therapy: Group therapy is also something you will encounter quite a bit of in treatment, or in any form of mental health treatment you pursue. Not only does it help you to come out of your shell while you're at your treatment center, but you get to know your fellow patients and may find that you have more in common with them than just sharing an eating or other co-occurring disorder. Many people feel hesitant when it comes to group therapy, as it can seem a little unnatural to have to share personal details about oneself. However, if you can encourage yourself to open up and share about your life—or just about your eating disorder—you may find that you are able to feel a bit more at home than you might have previously expected.
- Family Therapy: For many individuals, family therapy is a crucial part of the healing process. Unless your therapist specifies differently, one of your individual therapy sessions will usually be used for family therapy each week while you are in treatment. Family therapy, unlike other forms of therapy, is typically optional. It can help you grow closer to your family members and tackle some hidden (or not so hidden) issues that might be lurking, but you do not have to spend one of your individual sessions with your family unless you want to. However, it may assist you once you graduate from eating disorder treatment if your family is going to be part of your support team; they will need to know what to do to best be there for you, and those skills can be built in family therapy with the help of your therapist as a mediator.

- Equine Therapy: Equine therapy is not offered by every treatment center, but it is offered frequently enough that it is worth mentioning as a treatment option for you. If you like working with horses, or even think that it might be something you'd like to try, equine therapy could be for you. Some people are put-off or frightened by horses and large animals, but the horses that are chosen for equine therapy are gentle and used to being around anxious, depressed, or disabled humans. You will not always be riding horses during therapy, and depending on your medical state, you may never. Even so, you can still participate in therapy with the horses by brushing, feeding, and leading the horses in and out of obstacle courses.
- Yoga: Yoga is the one form of exercise, besides gentle walking, that you may be allowed to participate in while you are still in treatment. Some treatment centers provide a yoga class led by a certified yoga instructor, or, at the very least, they will put on a video for you to watch. There are many documented benefits to yoga, which is why so many treatment centers offer it as a form of movement and a reintroduction to what it means to be one with the body you have, as opposed to the body you might wish you had. Yoga can be quite slow and it may involve only gentle stretching, which can be a great way to learn how to exercise again without the intent to break out in a sweat and burn calories. It is about balance, mindfulness, and feeling at peace within yourself. If you have a meditation practice, yoga in treatment can be an excellent time to engage in it.
- Acupuncture/Acupressure: Acupuncture is a form of Eastern medicine that is offered at some treatment centers. In case you are not familiar with the term, acupuncture involves the gentle insertion of tiny, thin needles just underneath the first layer of skin along very specific areas on the body. In treatment, you may only have needles inserted on your ears, forehead, or hands rather than on the entire body, unless your treatment center offers full acupuncture treatments. If needles make you squeamish, you may also have the option for acupressure, which features tiny magnets instead of needles that can be pressed

along the body's pressure points to achieve the same purpose as the needles would. Acupressure has approximately the same health benefits as acupuncture, so don't force yourself to face your fear of needles unless you are feeling particularly brave and want to give it a shot.

We have examined, in depth, your various treatment options and have given you a taste of what going to residential treatment might be like. Now, it's time to meet Stella. Stella is another one of our volunteers who has graciously allowed you insight into her world. Perhaps your journey will look something like Stella's, or perhaps you will see nothing familiar here; as we know, each recovery journey is unique. Let's take a look now at what Stella has to share about her own.

Stella's Story

Stella has no memory of her parents ever having been together. They got divorced when she was only six months old, and although her mother wanted to try to see the relationship through, her father didn't, and simply left. As a result, Stella grew up very close to her mother, and describes their relationship as almost more of a sisterhood than a mother-daughter bond. Her mother had primary custody of her, and the two of them spent lots of time together. It was the way Stella liked things. As she puts it, her mom was her rock.

Stella grew up painfully shy, and began to show signs of obsessive compulsive disorder at age six. She was petrified of making eye contact with anyone, but she was chastised for it because her father was shy, and it came across as being rude. Despite her shyness, Stella always had straight A's in school, had many friends to play with, and kept up with a variety of extracurricular activities, including playing the violin, going to soccer practice, and attending summer camps and dance practices. By the time she got to middle school, Stella was doing everything she could to be more outgoing and less shy in order to avoid ending up like her father. However, it was at around this time in her life that she first began to feel unbeautiful. While all of the other girls in her classes seemed to be getting boyfriends and having their first kisses, Stella was "just this scrawny girl in a childlike body with glasses and braces." She felt ugly by comparison.

At around this time, both of Stella's parents got remarried, which only served to make middle school more uncomfortable for her. She found herself feeling jealous and angry when it came to her mother's new husband, and confused and blindsided by her father's new wife, as she didn't even know he'd had a girlfriend to begin with. She wasn't invited to her father's wedding for reasons that remain a mystery to her, and her parents, clearly sensing the turmoil she was in, put her in therapy for the first time to help her cope with the changes.

In high school, more changes occurred for Stella, some of them good, others less so. For one, she got her braces off and boys began to notice her for the first time. She was smart, played soccer and lacrosse, ran track, and could entertain any guy who showed interest in her. And yet she felt as though she were constantly living in her best friend's shadow, who was a nationally ranked athletic superstar who she felt was funnier and more beautiful than her. The two were a duo, but Stella felt as though she always came in second place, though she felt guilty for having those feelings in the first place. Her self-esteem started to dip, and she took refuge in seeking attention from male upperclassmen, which she did quite successfully. This marked the beginning of what would become a pattern of looking to men for validation, which would dog her for many years.

Also in high school, as one might expect with all of the sports she was doing, came the first of Stella's compulsive exercise habits. At the time, she had no idea that they were compulsive, which is the case for many eating disorder sufferers in the beginning. She was praised for her hard work by her coaches, which only served to reinforce her behavior. Her mental health began to take a turn in other ways when, in biology class, she had her first panic attack. Fearful that she would have another, she eventually created a self-fulfilling prophecy wherein she continued to have panic attacks in part because she was so afraid of having them, and, finally, she was diagnosed with anxiety and OCD. She was put on medication, which seemed to help.

Despite these hardships, Stella continued to stay on top of her studies and all of her extracurriculars, and was accepted into her dream school, Boston University. As soon as she arrived, she made friends with a group of girls on her floor, and it was a wonderful experience after having only one best friend to call her own in high school. She studied abroad in Europe for a time, and it was after this that she began to notice that her body had changed in ways that she wasn't very comfortable with. After spending that semester abroad and eating and drinking whatever made her happy, she had gained a little weight. Stella remembers the way she was traveling to an array of amazing countries, and all she could think about was how she was going to lose the weight she had gained when she was going to get back home. This was only made worse because all of her friends were doing exactly the same thing, so the fact that the body discomfort was a group activity made it even more all-encompassing.

When she did arrive back in the United States and got back to school, Stella's life resumed its normal course . . . for a while. She lost the weight she had gained, ran back into the arms of an on-again, off-again boyfriend, and kept seeing her friends. However, Stella's desire for male attention wound up getting the better of her, even though she didn't mean to cause any harm, and the result it had on her life was devastating. Her friendships ended, her boyfriend broke up with her, and she wound up being ostracized in her own apartment. She self-harmed for the first time, and when her roommate found out, she accused her of seeking attention and called her pathetic. Stella went from loving school to hating it, traveling home on the weekends whenever she could in order to spend as much time away from school as she was able. She felt isolated and completely alone . . . which set the stage for her eating disorder to swoop in and take the helm as a means of self-rescue.

Stella took refuge in the health and fitness blogs that Instagram provided, and met a girl who, despite being completely uncertified, offered to help her get fit and lose weight. As we learned in the previous chapter when we explored pro-ana and pro-mia websites, the internet can be a prime place for eating disorder sufferers to gather together and encourage one another's eating disorders to bloom, and is just what happened to Stella. Armed with a new diet and exercise regimen, Stella felt a new sense of purpose and belonging, one that she had lost when her friends had turned on her. She drew a sense of power and control from her restrictive eating patterns and began to compile a list of "safe" foods to eat, avoiding everything that wasn't on that list. She spent hours upon hours in the gym, and recalls that it was the one place she could be every day where she could "be alone, but not feel lonely." As college finally drew to an end, Stella's harmful behaviors had escalated into a full-blown eating disorder.

When she went home after school ended, Stella's weight loss and changes in behavior did not go unnoticed by her parents. They were concerned, but ultimately assumed that the difference in Stella was due to the stress of school. They were partially right, of course, but being home did not help her get better, and she only fell deeper into her eating disorder. She started weighing everything she ate, running for hours everyday, and avoiding mealtimes with her parents so she could stick to her "safe" foods. In her words, she was a skeleton of herself. But she didn't seek treatment. Not yet.

Stella started her first full-time job despite her eating disorder, which was rapidly progressing. She worked seventy hours a week, still managing to find time to wake up at four in the morning to exercise before work. She never ate and was utterly miserable. Her parents found her a therapist and a dietitian, seeing that she was in the throes of an eating disorder and doing little to hide it, but it wasn't enough. After a mere six months at her job, Stella had to quit to go to her first residential treatment facility in St. Louis. However, she was extremely resistant to treatment, compulsively exercised her way through, and relapsed as soon as she got home.

Relapse is a part of recovery for eating disorder sufferers, but Stella's relapse was particularly hard on her. She got sicker faster than before, and became even thinner. She moved in with a roommate in Boston, which gave her all the more freedom to run endlessly and never eat. Before she knew it, it was time to go back to treatment again, this time all the way in Florida at another residential treatment facility. Once again, she wasn't very excited to be there, and the way the place was run didn't make things any easier:

Once again, I was not pleased to be in treatment, and was pretty much doing it to make my parents stop worrying that I was going to die. Again, I compulsively exercised my entire stay, and me and my friends in treatment encouraged each other to hide food. They showed us our weight every morning, which led to my new extreme fixation on the number on the scale. The more it went up as I weight restored, the more I hated myself.

When Stella finished residential in Florida, she moved on to PHP in Boston, continuing to restore the weight she had lost and hating herself as she did so, and many people with eating disorders do. Her body recovered, but her mind did not. As the years went by, Stella continued to compulsively exercise and restrict, but tried to look "recovered" by eating socially and keeping up with her outpatient team, who were less pleased with her than the people in her life, with less knowledge, were. She even started running half and full marathons, which earned her plenty of praise, just as all of her extra running once had back in high school. And then COVID-19 struck, and things changed. Her eating disorder used the opportunity of being stuck in the house to ramp up her workouts, but nothing made her lose weight like she was accustomed to in the past, which she found frustrating. She became more rigid in her other eating disorder behaviors as a result, and began to spiral once again into her eating disorder instead of just coasting along like she had been for years. When she started to have bouts of extreme depression, she knew that things were heading for another all-time low. She stopped being able to exercise regularly, go to work, and feed herself. She knew that the people in her life who she cared about the most were starting to get worried, so she decided once and for all that it was time to beat her eating disorder, and checked herself into treatment of her own volition for the first time.

This round of treatment was a completely different experience for Stella. Not only did she go on her own, but almost everyone else at her treatment center had, too. This created a wholesome, recovery-oriented environment in which nearly everyone there was on the same page and could encourage each other through the tough moments. Stella also had a great relationship with her therapist, which truly made her time in treatment memorable—she felt like she mattered.

Today, Stella is overall doing quite well for herself. A move to a new city made her eating disorder want to pop back up again, but once she finished up with treatment, she was able to go back to her outpatient team, and they helped her through. Additionally, Stella has stopped running compulsively, and hasn't run since prior to going to treatment the last time—a massive accomplishment for her. She is also doing better all the time with trying new foods spontaneously, just like someone without an eating disorder would do. Stella is on the road to recovery, and even though her anxiety and OCD do sometimes make things difficult, she is doing her best.

Stella's story shows us that treatment can be a rocky experience, but that not all centers are the same and that in the end, our treatment experience is largely what we make of it. When she wasn't ready to recover and was in a center that was encouraging her behaviors by showing her weight, her treatment experience was miserable. But when she finally gave in to the process and knew that it was time to recover for good, she found herself surrounded by like-minded individuals who also wanted to recover, which made it that much easier to put herself on the right track. There are no morals to be drawn from anyone's recovery story—that's not what these testimonials are here for. But Stella's journey might give you insight into your own recovery—or that of a loved one's—and help you see that only you can take that first step.

If you are ready to take that first step, but aren't sure where to begin, some good treatment centers to start at may be Alsana, Center for Discovery, and The Eating Recovery Center, to name a few. Make sure you follow the steps we listed earlier in this chapter before settling on any one center, as eating disorder treatment can be pricey and you want to make sure that your insurance will cover it if you cannot afford to pay for it yourself. However, do keep in mind that your life is more important than your wallet, if that's what it comes down to, and treatment is always worth it if it gets you that much closer to living your life once again.

SIX

Intuitive Eating

INTUITIVE EATING IS its own type of nutrition, and there are entire books about it that go into far more depth on the subject than we will within this chapter. However, intuitive eating is often considered the end goal by a myriad of eating disorder treatment facilities, as well as by many eating disorder treatment professionals, so the basic principles of it are absolutely worth going over. Each of these principles can be found as well on the Original Intuitive Eating Pros website (www.intuitiveeating.org) if you find yourself curious and looking for more information.

What Is Intuitive Eating?

Intuitive eating is the notion that one eats when they are hungry, stops when they are full, and does not adhere to any particular diet culture phenomenon when it comes to controlling their weight. They eat relatively healthfully, but do not stress about health—or weight—and focus instead on eating what makes both their taste buds and their body feel best. Intuitive eating is not a diet and it isn't about changing one's shape or size. In fact, it is a rejection of these things; it is freedom from diet culture and embracing, once more, how we were born knowing how to eat.

What Are the Principles of Intuitive Eating?

1. Reject the Diet Mentality: In this phase, it is time to throw away any diet magazines, cookbooks, diet foods, or other diet materials that you might have been using to try to keep yourself slim. More importantly, it's also time to get angry and indignant that the industry led you to want to use those things in the first place. In truth, you don't need any of those things to be fit, trim, happy, or anything in between, though, again, intuitive eating isn't about changing your body.

2. Honor Your Hunger: Next, you must learn once again how to listen to your hunger. This can be extraordinarily difficult for eating disorder sufferers, and you or your loved one may need guidance in order to help get it happening again. After starving or binging or both for a long period of time, it can be difficult to remember what it was like to be truly full or hungry, and there are physical processes that occur in the body that make this even more difficult to determine. However, this is a key step in learning how to eat intuitively, and you need to relearn how to feel your hunger cues if you are going to recover.

3. Make Peace with Food: Now, you must give up on giving up. No more forbidden foods or categorizing foods as "good" and "bad." This can lead to fear around eating and—when we finally do give in to a food we've been desperately wanting to taste—immense guilt and self-hatred, as well as binging. It's crucial that no foods ever be considered off-limits again, and that your war with food comes to an end.

4. Challenge the Food Police: The "food police" are a metaphor for the negative self-talk and diet beliefs that are ripe in eating disorder sufferers (and dieters). In order to combat your eating disorder, it is necessary to also chase away the food police. If it helps you to picture what the food police are, they are the intuitive eating version of "Ed," which is the abbreviation and personification that many people give their eating disorder. Whatever you call these diet beliefs and negative thoughts you need to work with a dietitian and therapist simultaneously to defeat them, and use the support of your friends and family to keep you on track when you need help.

5. Discover the Satisfaction Factor: With this principle, you may learn something new: how to be satisfied with food. Western cultures, often prepossessed by thinness and diets and other toxic concepts, are sometimes strangers to the notion that one can eat to be satisfied and not just to be full in a utilitarian way. To heal your eating disorder, you must learn how to make peace with the idea that food can be just as delicious as it is nutritious. Not only does this serve a purpose, but it can also be much more fun than eating just to survive.

6. Feel Your Fullness: Just as you must honor your hunger cues, you must learn to respect your fullness as well. This means that you eat only until you are comfortably full, knowing that you can always eat again later and that there is no need to stuff yourself or binge; the food will always be there later when you want or need it now that you are giving yourself the grace to eat. Being full may seem uncomfortable or even strange at first if you have been denying yourself the feeling for a while, but keep in mind that it's just a physical sensation that will go away over time.

7. Cope with Your Emotions with Kindness: Here, it becomes important to realize that there is a connection between how we are feeling and how we are eating. Whether you are restricting, binging, purging, or a mixture of the three (or have other behaviors to contend with), chances are that there is an emotional reason behind how you are coping with food. As we have learned, eating disorders are diseases of the mind and are connected to many different behaviors and emotions, and making peace with those emotions can be key in bringing an eating disorder to its knees.

8. Respect Your Body: This is a particularly difficult facet of intuitive eating for those with eating disorders. It is the part where you must stop trying to alter your body through diets and overexercising, and you must begin to embrace your natural body type, no matter what shape or size it is. This can seem unfair or even terrifying, but it is essential to the recovery process that you stop fighting and start allowing yourself to look how you look without feeling ashamed (though that part may come later).

9. Movement—Feel the Difference: It's time to stop trying to exercise to burn calories and start moving just to improve how you physically feel in yourself. Move gently—or less gently, if you are truly and honestly passionate about it, but wait until you are far along in your recovery process before implementing more extreme forms of movement again—and take note of how you like it. Do you enjoy exercising? Or have you been doing it for all of the wrong reasons? Take stock of your reasons for moving before setting out to do it, and only move in ways that make you the happiest.

10. Honor Your Health—Gentle Nutrition: Finally, eat to be healthy to the best of your ability, but don't stress about it! This means that you can have delicious foods that are healthy . . . or that are less so, too. It's all about balance and moderation, and about treating your body as well as you can without making it the end of the world if you want to have a slice of chocolate cake.[1]

Intuitive eating was not created for people with eating disorders, but it is a wonderful goal for those afflicted with them to shoot for when recovering. It can remind sufferers what it was like prior to the onset of their disorder, and create a solid aspiration and something to hope for again in the future.

During this brief chapter, we visited each principle of intuitive eating, and took you through each of them in detail. With luck, you now have a better idea of what life can be like without a diet or—worse yet—an eating disorder clouding your relationship with food. Now, it's time to meet Natasha. Natasha's story serves as an account of what it is like to go from being body-conscious, to having disordered eating behaviors, to having a full-blown eating disorder in a matter of years. If you see any similarities between Natasha's story and your own or someone in your life, be sure you seek out help as soon as possible, just as we always recommend.

Natasha's Story

When Natasha was little, her sister used to call her "fat" to push her buttons, despite the fact that Natasha was never on the large side. She was always taller than her older sister, and was told from a young age that she had her mother's body. This would have been an innocent enough thing to remark on if her mother had in any way been satisfied with the way that she looked. But her mother constantly complained about her legs, fretted that she needed to lose a certain number of pounds, and would come up with ways that she might go about doing so. Sometimes, it was that she would stop snacking after dinner, and other times, it was that she would cut out sugar entirely. However, at least to Natasha's knowledge, her mother never tried to manipulate her weight, with the exception of one two-day period during which she heavily restricted her calories, then went back to eating normally for the rest of the week. It's fair to say that Natasha was exposed to some less-than-healthy body image and approaches to eating at an early age.

Natasha's first instance of intentionally restricting her food for the purpose of losing weight happened in the seventh grade. She stopped eating lunch at school when she discovered that she was slowly gaining weight, which she now realizes was because she was still growing. During a routine trip to the doctor's office, she was weighed and consequently threatened to be sent to a treatment center for "skinny girls that don't eat." She used this encounter as an excuse to allow herself to eat lunch again, but notes that she came away from the experience without any idea as to what an eating disorder was.

Natasha describes herself as a very active child growing up. She signed up for club soccer when she was eight, but it was when she was eleven and started swimming that she had truly found the sport for her. By the time she was in eighth grade, she was practicing thirteen hours a week, and she loved her body, though she admits that this was a short-lived phenomenon. It was at around this time that she became preoccupied with the shape and size of her legs, and felt that she just *had* to have a "thigh gap." She also started to have binge urges around hyperpalatable foods in situations where she was presented with the opportunity to overconsume. For instance, she began volunteering at a horse ranch on Sundays, and there was a table of donuts, bagels, and chips. She frequently overate and would return home feeling bloated and ashamed. The same story took place at restaurants, dinner parties, and other situations when she was given full reign to eat. These urges didn't overtake her often enough to affect her weight, but it was enough to affect her self-esteem and how she saw herself.

Finally, Natasha became fed up with her binging one night after overconsuming her family's homemade macaroni and cheese. She felt ashamed for not respecting her fullness cues, and felt compelled to purge for the first time. She stuck the end of a toothbrush down her throat, but nothing happened, and her shame doubled. She was even more regretful afterwards, because she felt as though she couldn't even purge correctly—a truly worthless feeling for someone who was already feeling desperately low.

In ninth grade, Natasha hit her first depressive spell. She became a ghost of her former self, and felt isolated and incredibly lonely. She stopped attending swim practice regularly, if at all, and lost interest in all of the things that she had once enjoyed. She recalls a particular instance in which her mother caught her watching a show on her computer in her room and snacking, to which her mother reacted by ripping the snacks out of her hands and warning Natasha that she couldn't eat so much if she wasn't going to exercise. So, Natasha started playing water polo, and it actually helped her mood improve.

It was during Natasha's senior year that the restriction made a comeback. On top of water polo practice, her coach implemented crossfit and weight training twice a week, which caused Natasha to lose some weight and become a little more muscular despite her poor eating habits. She was still struggling with overeating, particularly after school when no one was home but her. She would go to practice afterwards feeling bloated and full, but she would leave with a flat stomach after working hard and burning off her binge.

After the season ended, Natasha joined a gym in order to keep her fitness on track, but it wasn't the same as the workouts she was putting in while she was on her water polo team. She continued to struggle with her eating habits, and the hours she put in at the gym couldn't compare to how much she had been exercising before. So, before she knew it, she had gained a few pounds, and she hated how she felt and looked. She started trying to diet to lean out and keep her abs defined, which she had always been able to see when she was on the water polo team, but she was never able to stick to her goals.

In September of 2018, Natasha went off to college, and she recalls feeling like "a complete mess." Her eating disorder flourished here, and took off in full swing. Natasha describes her eating disorder the following way:

Since the first day of school, I logged every bit of food I ate. My fitness pal set my calorie total for the day, and I stuck to it like it was a religion. I joined the club swim team, and made a commitment to the gym. For the majority of my freshman year, I went to the gym every morning Monday through Friday, walked anywhere from six to ten miles a day, and practiced with the swim team every night Monday through Saturday. I meticulously counted calories and labeled foods "good" and "bad." I jumped on the protein hype, thinking that protein bars were the holy grail of all foods. To this day I have a weird relationship with protein bars.

And then things took a turn for the worse. Natasha contracted a virus that affected her ability to breathe, so she was no longer able to practice as consistently as she used to with the swim team. She started to grow weaker at the gym, and her frustration with her body increased as her strength dwindled. By the end of the school year, she knew that there was something wrong, so she started looking up her symptoms online and getting lab work done. Sure enough, it was looking more and more like she had an eating disorder, but she was unwilling to ask for the help she needed. Eating disorders, as we know, are secretive, and Natasha wanted to try to heal herself on her own. So she tried.

In short, it did not go well. The following year was nothing but more binging, restricting, and overexercising. Looking back, Natasha now knows that fixing one behavior doesn't equal fixing an eating disorder; she held on to her food rules and continued to deteriorate into a binge-restrict cycle that had her starting a new behavior: night eating. She would wake up in the wee hours of the morning to have a meal, then feel so guilty the next morning that she would starve herself until noon and overexercise to compensate, only to restart the cycle again. Her roommate helped her brainstorm ideas to keep her out of the kitchen at night, and they decided that Natasha would try to stay up as late as possible so she would be too tired to get up and eat. Unfortunately, this just altered her already-disturbed sleep schedule, and it caused her to feel depressed to the point of having suicidal thoughts. When she went home in May, she broke up with her boyfriend, one of the only people she felt comforted by. By the end of July, she missed him, but after having a talk with one of her closest friends, she got a dietitian instead of getting back together.

This time, Natasha was willing to admit to herself that she had an eating disorder, and that she couldn't handle it on her own. She called her parents and talked to them about it, then found a therapist and, of course, her dietitian to help her start her recovery. Her dietitian was able to get her to break some of her food rules, and Natasha's night eating ground to a stop. During this time, she felt good about her recovery . . . and then things got tense with her college roommate, and that changed. The restriction and night eating returned, and Natasha began to feel out of control again. Her mental health began to deteriorate once again, and by the time November arrived, Natasha was suicidal once more. Her eating disorder had her in a vice, and she felt frustrated just to be alive. She took a trip to visit her ex, and the entire time she found herself hyperfocused on the intuitive way he was eating. She was jealous of how he could just eat, and exhausted by the way she just couldn't.

Her mood had improved a little over the course of the trip, but when she got back to college, Natasha was depressed again. Her eating disorder continued to consume her, and her night eating behaviors got worse. There were times when she would get up at night and realize she was in the kitchen without knowing how she had gotten there. She felt too overwhelmed by grocery stores to go shopping for food, and her self-hatred was overpowering. She felt like she was "drowning." Finally, in January, Natasha had to start seeing another dietitian because her old one just couldn't help her night eating behaviors. She came clean about her deep depression and her fears about falling deeper into it, as well as all of her behaviors. Treatment followed shortly thereafter.

Now, Natasha is doing quite well. Her emotional state is much better now that she is feeding herself in a way that is in line with what her body truly needs, and she is happier. The word *health* has a completely different meaning for her than it once did, and in a good way: now it means something more akin to balance. For example, there was a time in Natasha's life when she would have thought of a granola bar as a "useless" food, and wouldn't have touched it. Now, she enjoys them and sees the merit in them simply because they are convenient and she likes the taste, and not everything has to be about foods being perfect. All in all, Natasha is well on the way to recovering from her eating disorder, and her story to date has a happy ending.

Natasha is thriving and using some of her own intuitive eating principles as she lives out her life, and, clearly, is doing rather well for herself. If you're curious about intuitive eating and want to know more, you can either visit the Original Intuitive Eating Pros website (www.intuitiveeating.org) from the beginning of this chapter or, better yet, read the intuitive eating book that many dietitians give their eating disorder clients: *Intuitive Eating: A Revolutionary Program that Works* by Evelyn Tribole and Elyse Resch. It will give you all the guidance you need on the subject, and help you on your first steps toward a brighter, eating disorder–free future, particularly if you are just starting your recovery journey.

SEVEN

Is Recovery Possible?

IN PART, we have used the recovery stories at the end of every chapter to illustrate our stance that, indeed, recovery is possible for every eating disorder sufferer and that it is never too late to seek help for your behaviors. Not each and every one of our stories ended as a fairytale would, but they are far from sad, hopeless, or distressing; they are simply distinctive and unique, as the people who lived them are. They are all on different roads toward their own recoveries, and, as no two recoveries look quite the same (as we know), they will all get there in their own time.

So, will you or your loved one be able to get to "recovered" someday? Unfortunately, the answer is one that you may not want to hear, which is that it completely depends on the individual, *and* that the experts disagree. Some will argue that you can fully recover from an eating disorder after plenty of therapy and hard work, but others will say that you may be faced with triggers and eating disorder thoughts for the rest of your life. The truth may lie somewhere in between, but at least with the men and women we've observed so far, it looks as though it is possible to have a bright future even with an eating disorder in your past. You can still live the life you want to even if you have occasional eating disorder thoughts.

What Is the Difference Between *Recovery* and *Recovered*?

For the majority of this book, we have been focusing primarily on the *recovery* process and not so much on the endpoint, mainly because not everyone agrees that there is an endpoint. This endpoint, should it exist, would be when you are officially *recovered*. We'll explore the difference between being *in recovery* and being *recovered* below.

- Being in recovery: When you are in recovery, there is not necessarily an end in sight. Depending on what your eating disorder looks like and how it has shaped you, it may be a long, long state, which is perfectly alright: many people who suffer from addiction also refer to themselves as being *in recovery* when they are doing well and staying on track, and this can be the case for you, too, if you wish. For an eating disorder, however, being in recovery means that you are working on developing the necessary tools to keep your eating disorder at bay while also restoring your physical health. It can also mean that you are having a relapse, as relapse can be part of the recovery journey and does not mean you have failed—it just means you are still in that *in recovery* phase. Remember not to put a time frame on the recovery stage; even though it can be frustrating and you may want to rush straight

through to being recovered, doing the work is the best way to get there. Putting more constraints on yourself isn't.
- Being recovered: Being recovered is the goal for any eating disorder treatment professional who believes that such a thing is possible—and it can be your goal, too, if you like. When you are recovered, apart from the memories you have and the fact that you will likely want to continue with therapy just to make sure your skills stay sharp, it may be like you never had an eating disorder. In theory, you will be eating intuitively again, your relationship with exercise will have returned to normal, and you will be free from the rigidity and obsessiveness that may have come to rule your life. You will need to accept your natural body shape and size in order to get to this point, no matter how it changes throughout your recovery.

It is important to recognize that not even the definitions of what *recovery* is are always fully agreed upon. To some experts, someone is in recovery for the rest of their lives, and that encapsulates the *recovered* phase. To others, being recovered means that the eating disorder must no longer have any impact whatsoever on the individual.[1] Whatever the case is for you, realize that you are far from alone in this process, and that even if the experts can't agree on whether or not recovery is possible, one thing is for certain: it doesn't start getting better until you reach out for assistance for you or your loved one, and take that first step toward whatever recovery looks like for you.

Finally, it's time to meet one last volunteer who has kindly offered to share his story with you. His tale is somewhat unlike all of the rest of those we've met with eating disorders up to this point, so if you are struggling to find a place where you fit in, perhaps you will be able to find commonalities with Colin. As always, if you do start to check boxes and see that you have some behaviors that are one in the same, reach out for help as soon as you can. Recovery starts with you and it does get better.

Colin's Story

Colin's story is a little different than the others we have been introduced to so far. For one, his eating disorder has always fallen more comfortably under the category of disordered eating than a full-blown eating disorder, but that doesn't mean that he has struggled any less than the women and men we've met up to this point. Colin's main sources of woe lie not necessarily in food, but in body image and his thought processes about how he sees himself, and in the past, that blossomed into the eating disorder behaviors that got him into trouble.

Unlike some people who battle with eating disorder behaviors, Colin's disordered eating didn't start in childhood. However, he was raised by a family who was body-conscious, particularly his mother, who Colin suspects has disordered eating—if not an eating disorder—of her own. She isn't to blame for Colin's disordered eating, as no one can cause another person to develop an eating disorder. However, the fact remains that Colin's eating disorder behaviors began to emerge when he was in college, though, when he reflects back, he can't quite remember why it happened.

When he was enjoying himself in school, like many people, Colin gained weight. He can't remember whether or not someone in his family commented on it first, but the end result was the same: for the first time in his life, Colin became more conscious of his body in a way that he was increasingly uncomfortable with, and it stuck with him. This is the way that Colin's disordered eating primarily presents itself: as poor body image that he can feel in a very visceral, physical way. He became hyperaware of his weight, of the way it felt to be in his body, of the way his stomach was positioned while he was sitting down—all of these details haunted him until he finally began skipping meals and restricting what he ate. This all occurred in approximately 2015, and the effect it had on his body was swift. He lost a noticeable amount of weight, so much so that his family began to praise him for it. He learned that being thin was a good thing, and he strove to never let it go again.

And so it went on for the next several years. A typical day in Colin's life wasn't exactly food-focused and it didn't necessarily revolve around how his body looked, but the eating disorder behaviors were always there, lurking in the background. He weighed himself every day, if not every other day, and if the number went up, he was flooded with a sense of anxiety and dread. No matter what, he did not want to be "fat," and he did not want to allow the number on the scale to exceed a certain limit. If it did, he knew that he needed to cut back more. And Colin already was cutting back. He only allowed himself to eat two meals a day, skipping lunch entirely and replacing it with a small snack if he had to eat anything at all. Occasionally, he permitted himself to enjoy dessert after dinner with his family, depending on what he had eaten and how much, but if he had eaten more than a certain amount, then dessert was out the window. And then, in 2021, Colin met his boyfriend, and things started to change.

Colin's boyfriend, like Colin, struggles with his eating. Unlike Colin, however, Colin's boyfriend has been in and out of treatment centers and has struggled with a full-blown eating disorder rather than disordered eating behaviors. Rather than encourage each other's behaviors like you might expect, Colin and his boyfriend worked to help each other heal. They met while Colin's boyfriend was still in treatment for a different disorder, and, by and by, Colin was rather forcibly taught how to start eating again. He reinstated lunch at his boyfriend's request, but the result of this was that he began to gain back healthy weight again as his body approached its set point. Colin, completely new to the concept of set points, panicked and feared that the weight would continue to pile on forever. Fortunately, his boyfriend reassured him that it wouldn't and taught him some of the skills he had learned in treatment, and life marched on.

Today, Colin still has times when his body image hits an all-time low, but he continues to eat. He refuses to restrict, so he weighs more than he is comfortable with, which can be difficult for him when he is having a particularly rough day. His brain will still lie to him and tell him that his body is larger than it really is, but he still has his boyfriend by his side to let him know that it's all in his head. Colin threw out his scale about two months ago and no longer weighs himself, and he doesn't miss it.

Colin's tale is a little different because he never went to treatment like the other people we've met, but that doesn't negate his hardships or make them any less meaningful in his journey to a healthier, happier life. In fact, he is working on assembling an outpatient team for himself that would include a psychiatrist and a dietitian in addition to his current therapist and physician. All in all, Colin is doing well for himself, and is on the road to a full recovery, despite the occasional rough day or moment that still visits him.

Colin's story shows us that recovery is possible, even for people who do not have eating disorder stories that carry them all the way through to inpatient or residential treatment. Not all eating disorders—whether they are full-on eating disorders, are closer to disordered eating, or are somewhere in between—are cookie-cutter shapes that can all have predictable beginnings, middles, and ends. As we have learned, recovery isn't necessarily linear, and even though it has been so far for Colin, that doesn't mean that it will be for you or your loved one, and there is no shame in that. It's likely that Colin will continue to improve with the help of his outpatient team and boyfriend, and you, or your loved one with an eating disorder, are fully capable of doing the same.

Final Words

Eating disorders do not discriminate.

If those words sound familiar to you, they likely should: they were how we opened the introduction of our book. They ring just as true now as they did back at the beginning, though perhaps now you have a slightly better grasp of just what they mean for you or your loved one with an eating disorder.

Throughout the course of this book, we learned what an eating disorder is, as well as discussed each of the known types of eating disorders in-depth. We looked at the causes, and looked at who gets eating disorders (which, if you recall, can be any of us—this is why the words "eating disorders do not discriminate" ring so true). We explored treatment options and took you on a tour through a day in the life at a residential treatment facility, just to give you a better idea of the options that are out there. Finally, we took a compendious view of intuitive eating and briefly encountered the question of whether or not recovery is possible. We also provided resources for you to use if you need more information or are currently struggling.

If you take away one thing from this book, let it be that despite what an expert here or there might tell you, becoming fully recovered is absolutely a goal worth striving for . . . but you are unlikely to do it alone. You may not need to head to a treatment center to get the help you need for you or your loved one's eating disorder, but, just as Natasha learned, it can be enormously difficult to go at it alone when it comes to trying to get better. Do not be afraid to reach out to someone you trust. You may save a life.

Finally, a special thank you to the volunteers who made the testimonials at the end of each chapter possible. Without you, this would have been a much different book, and, with luck, the generous donation of your stories will reach someone and prompt them to get them the help they need. Thank you.

References

Introduction.

1. "What Are Eating Disorders?" National Eating Disorders Association [Webpage], n.d., https://www.nationaleatingdisorders.org/what-are-eating-disorders.

2. Jon Arcelus, Alex J. Mitchell, and Jackie Wales, "Mortality Rates in Patients with Anorexia Nervosa and Other Eating Disorders. A Meta-Analysis of 36 Studies," *Arch Gen Psychiatry* 68(7), July 2011, 724–731. https://doi.org/10.1001/archgenpsychiatry.2011.74.

Chapter One.

1. "What Are Eating Disorders?" American Psychiatric Association [Webpage], March 2021, https://www.psychiatry.org/patients-families/eating-disorders/what-are-eating-disorders.

2. *Diagnostic and Statistical Manual of Mental Disorders* (5th ed.), American Psychiatric Association, 2013, https://doi.org/10.1176/appi.books.9780890425596.

3. *Diagnostic and Statistical Manual*, 2013.

4. "Anorexia Nervosa," National Eating Disorders Association [Webpage], n.d., https://www.nationaleatingdisorders.org/learn/by-eating-disorder/anorexia.

5. "Anorexia Nervosa," NEDA, n.d.

6. "Anorexia Nervosa," NEDA, n.d.

7. Bridget Engel, "Characteristics of Anorexia Nervosa," Gulf Bend Center [Webpage], n.d., https://www.gulfbend.org/poc/view_doc.php?type=doc&id=11756&cn=46.

8. "Health Consequences," National Eating Disorders Association [Webpage], n.d., https://www.nationaleatingdisorders.org/health-consequences.

9. *Diagnostic and Statistical Manual*, 2013.

10. "Bulimia Nervosa," National Eating Disorders Association [Webpage], n.d., https://www.nationaleatingdisorders.org/learn/by-eating-disorder/bulimia.

11. "Bulimia Nervosa," NEDA, n.d.

12. "Bulimia Nervosa," NEDA, n.d.

13. "Bulimia Nervosa," NEDA, n.d.

14. Sara Altshul, "What It Feels Like to Have Binge Eating Disorder," *Everyday Health*, June 21, 2016, https://www.everydayhealth.com/eating-disorders/living-with/what-it-feels-like-have-binge-eating-disorder/.

15. *Diagnostic and Statistical Manual*, 2013.

16. "Binge Eating Disorder," National Eating Disorders Association [Webpage], n.d., https://www.nationaleatingdisorders.org/learn/by-eating-disorder/bed.

17. "Binge Eating Disorder," NEDA, n.d.

18. "What Does Compulsive Overeating Feel Like?" The Emily Program [Webpage], February 20, 2020, https://www.emilyprogram.com/blog/what-does-compulsive-overeating-feel-like/.

19. "Binge Eating Disorder," NEDA, n.d.

20. "Binge Eating Disorder Health Risks," Walden Behavioral Care [Webpage], n.d., https://www.waldeneatingdisorders.com/what-we-treat/binge-eating-disorder/binge-eating-disorder-health-risks/.

21. Keith Delvin, "Top 10 Reasons Why the BMI Is Bogus," *NPR*, July 4, 2009, https://www.npr.org/templates/story/story.php?storyId=106268439.

22. Marci Anderson, "What Is Disordered Eating?" Academy of Nutrition and Dietetics: Eat Right [Blog], October 26, 2018, reviewed February 2020, https://www.eatright.org/health/diseases-and-conditions/eating-disorders/what-is-disordered-eating.

23. "Anorexia Nervosa," Cleveland Clinic [Webpage], reviewed June 27, 2019, https://my.clevelandclinic.org/health/diseases/9794-anorexia-nervosa

24. "Anorexia Nervosa," Cleveland Clinic, 2019.

25. "Bulimia Nervosa," Cleveland Clinic [Webpage], reviewed December 12, 2019, https://my.clevelandclinic.org/health/diseases/9795-bulimia-nervosa

26. Roxanne Dryden-Edwards, "Binge Eating Disorder," MedicineNet [Webpage], reviewed March 16, 2021, https://www.medicinenet.com/binge_eating_disorder/article.htm.

27. "Anorexia Nervosa," Cleveland Clinic, 2019.

28. "Anxiety, Depression, & Obsessive Compulsive Disorder," National Eating Disorders Association [Webpage], n.d., https://www.nationaleatingdisorders.org/anxiety-depression-obsessive-compulsive-disorder.

29. "What Is Obsessive Compulsive Disorder?" American Psychiatric Association [Webpage], reviewed December 2020, https://www.psychiatry.org/patients-families/ocd/what-is-obsessive-compulsive-disorder#:~:text=Obsessive%2Dcompulsive%20disorder%20(OCD)%20is%20a%20disorder%20in%20which,do%20something%20repetitively%20(compulsions).

30. "Substance Abuse and Eating Disorders," National Eating Disorders Association [Webpage], n.d., https://www.nationaleatingdisorders.org/substance-abuse-and-eating-disorders.

31. "Substance Abuse and Eating Disorders," NEDA, n.d.

Chapter Two.

1. "Other Specified Feeding or Eating Disorder," National Eating Disorders Association [Webpage], n.d., https://www.nationaleatingdisorders.org/learn/by-eating-disorder/osfed.

2. "What Is Purging Disorder?" MedicineNet [Webpage], reviewed December 3, 2019, https://www.medicinenet.com/purging_disorders/article.htm.

3. "Other Specified Feeding and Eating Disorders (OSFED)," National Eating Disorders Collaboration [Webpage], n.d., https://nedc.com.au/

eating-disorders/eating-disorders-explained/types/other-specified-feeding-or-eating-disorders/.

4. David Steen Martin, "What Is Night Eating Syndrome?" *WebMD*, reviewed May 17, 2021, https://www.webmd.com/mental-health/eating-disorders/binge-eating-disorder/what-is-night-eating-syndrome.

5. "OSFED," National Eating Disorders Association [Webpage], n.d., https://www.nationaleatingdisorders.org/learn/by-eating-disorder/osfed.

6. "OSFED," NEDA, n.d.

7. "OSFED," NEDA, n.d.

8. Eating Recovery Center. (2021, October 17). "Health Risks for Other Eating Disorders (OSFED)."https://www.eatingrecoverycenter.com/conditions/osfed/health-risks.

9. "Health Risks of Other Eating Disorders (OSFED)," Eating Recovery Center [Webpage], n.d., https://www.eatingrecoverycenter.com/conditions/osfed/health-risks.

10. "Orthorexia," National Eating Disorders Association [Webpage], n.d., https://www.nationaleatingdisorders.org/learn/by-eating-disorder/other/orthorexia.

11. "Orthorexia," NEDA, n.d.

12. "Orthorexia," NEDA, n.d.

13. Alina Petre, "Orthorexia: When Healthy Eating Becomes a Disorder," *Healthline*, April 2, 2020, https://www.healthline.com/nutrition/orthorexia-nervosa-101.

14. *Diagnostic and Statistical Manual*, 2013.

15. "ARFID Signs & Symptoms," Center for Discovery [Webpage], n.d., https://centerfordiscovery.com/conditions/arfid/.

16. "Avoidant Restrictive Food Intake Disorder (ARFID)," National Eating Disorders Association [Webpage], n.d., https://www.nationaleatingdisorders.org/learn/by-eating-disorder/arfid.

17. "Avoidant Restrictive Food Intake Disorder," NEDA, n.d.

18. "Avoidant Restrictive Food Intake Disorder," NEDA, n.d.

19. "Avoidant Restrictive Food Intake Disorder," NEDA, n.d.

20. "ARFID Signs & Symptoms," Center for Discover, n.d.

21. "Avoidant Restrictive Food Intake Disorder," NEDA, n.d.

22. "What Is Pica?" Family Doctor [Webpage], updated January 28, 2021, https://familydoctor.org/condition/pica/.

23. "Pica," National Eating Disorders Association [Webpage], n.d., https://www.nationaleatingdisorders.org/learn/by-eating-disorder/other/pica.

24. Diagnostic and Statistical Manual, 2013.

25. "Pica," NEDA, n.d.

26. "What Is Pica?" Family Doctor, 2021.

27. "Pica," NEDA, n.d.

28. "What Is Pica?" Family Doctor, 2021.

29. "Pica," NEDA, n.d.

30. "Diabulimia," National Eating Disorders Association, n.d., https://www.nationaleatingdisorders.org/diabulimia-5.

31. "Diabulimia," NEDA, n.d.

32. "Diabulimia," NEDA, n.d.

33. "Diabulimia," NEDA, n.d.

34. "Diabulimia," NEDA, n.d.

35. "Diabulimia," NEDA, n.d.

36. "Rumination Syndrome," Mayo Clinic [Webpage], October 14, 2020. https://www.mayoclinic.org/diseases-conditions/rumination-syndrome/symptoms-causes/syc-20377330.

37. *Diagnostic and Statistical Manual*, 2013.

38. "Rumination Syndrome," Mayo Clinic, 2020.

39. "Rumination Syndrome," Mayo Clinic, 2020.

40. "Rumination Syndrome," Mayo Clinic, 2020.

Chapter Three.

1. Libby Lyons, "Genetic Factors Behind Eating Disorders," Eating Disorder Hope [Blog], March 19, 2017, https://www.eatingdisorderhope.com/blog/genetic-factors-eating-disorders.

2. Lyons, Eating Disorder Hope, 2017.

3. Gina Shaw, "Anorexia and Bulimia: Cracking the Genetic Code," *WebMD*, n.d., https://www.webmd.com/mental-health/eating-disorders/anorexia-nervosa/features/anorexia-bulimia-genetic-code.

4. Bridget Engel, "Causes of Eating Disorders—Biological Factors," Gulf Bend Center [Webpage], n.d., https://www.gulfbend.org/poc/view_doc.php?type=doc&id=11748&cn=46.

5. Engel, "Causes of Eating Disorders," Gulf Bend Center, n.d.

6. "Causes of Eating Disorders—Biological Factors," Mental Help [Webpage], n.d., https://www.mentalhelp.net/eating-disorders/causes-and-biological-factors/.

7. Lauren Muhlheim, "The Different Causes of Eating Disorders," *Very Well Mind*, updated January 5, 2021, https://www.verywellmind.com/what-causes-eating-disorders-4121047/.

8. Muhlheim, *Very Well Mind*, 2021.

9. Muhlheim, *Very Well Mind*, 2021.

Chapter Four.

1. "What Is an Eating Disorder?" Kelty Mental Health Resource Centre [Webpage], n.d., https://keltyeatingdisorders.ca/generalinformation/who-is-affected-by-eating-disorders/.

2. "What Is an Eating Disorder?" Kelty Mental Health Resource Centre, n.d.

3. Shereen Marisol Meraji, "When It Comes to Race, Eating Disorders Don't Discriminate," *NPR*, March 3, 2019, https://www.npr.org/sections/health-shots/2019/03/03/699410379/when-it-comes-to-race-eating-disorders-dont-discriminate.

4. "Eating Disorder Statistics," South Carolina Department of Mental Health [Webpage], n.d., https://www.state.sc.us/dmh/anorexia/statistics.htm.

5. "Eating Disorder Statistics," South Carolina DMH, n.d.

6. "People of Color and Eating Disorders," National Eating Disorders Association [Webpage], n.d., https://www.nationaleatingdisorders.org/people-color-and-eating-disorders.

7. Honor Whiteman, "Why Are Women More Vulnerable to Eating Disorders? Brain Study Sheds Light," *Medical News Today*, October 16, 2016, https://www.medicalnewstoday.com/articles/313466.

8. Jacquelyn Ekern, "Male Eating Disorders: A Snapshot of Statistics and Their Implications," Eating Disorder Hope [Blog], May 8, 2015, https://www.eatingdisorderhope.com/information/eating-disorder/male-eating-disorders-a-snapshot-of-statistics-and-their-implications.

9. "Eating Disorders in LGBTQ+ Populations," National Eating Disorders Association [Webpage], n.d., https://www.nationaleatingdisorders.org/learn/general-information/lgbtq.

Chapter Five.

1. "Eating Disorder Treatment: Know Your Options," Mayo Clinic [Webpage], July 14, 2017, https://www.mayoclinic.org/diseases-conditions/eating-disorders/in-depth/eating-disorder-treatment/art-20046234.

Chapter Six.

1. "10 Principles of Intuitive Eating," The Original Intuitive Eating Pros [Webpage], n.d., https://www.intuitiveeating.org/10-principles-of-intuitive-eating/.

Chapter Seven.

Carrie Hunnicutt, "Fully Recovered vs. In Recovery: A Discussion of the Similarities and Differences," Monte Nido [Webpage], n.d., https://www.montenido.com/fully-recovered-vs-in-recovery//.

Printed in Great Britain
by Amazon